Gustav Klimt

Author: Jane Rogoyska and Patrick Bade

Designed by:
Baseline Co Ltd
61A-63A Vo Van Tan Street
4th Floor
District 3, Ho Chi Minh City
Vietnam

ISBN: 978-1-84484-904-8

Printed in China

Jane Rogoyska and Patrick Bade

Gustav Klimt

PARKSTONE
INTERNATIONAL

Gustav Klimt

Contents

The Viennese Secession   7

His Life   19

His Work   63

Biography   192

Index   194

The Viennese Secession

Eight Years of Secession (March 1897 – June 1905)[1]
Criticism – Polemic Pamphlet – Chronicle
by Ludwig Hevesi, Vienna 1906

The city council has, in recent days, in a moment of epiphany, made the decision to grant the Vereinigung bildender Künstler Österreichs (Association of Visual Artists in Austria) a piece of property for the construction of an art exhibition center on the corner of the *Wollzeile* in Vienna[2]. The conditions, however, for this grant still need mitigation. This is what the Viennese would call a "Wiener Lokalnachricht" (a local headline) but compared to all the other headlines that have been published in the papers over the last years, this announcement is of tremendous importance. A magic word has been spoken which shall break the chains and raise the dead from their graves: an urban expansion is on the horizon that shall rejuvenate Vienna's art scene. As a city of the arts, Vienna, this formidable little town shall finally become Great Vienna, truly a New Vienna. The citizens of Vienna themselves are going to be surprised by the news since all the conspirators behind this project have been untiringly working in deepest silence in their metaphorical mountain retreat. The time of planning is finally over; today action speaks louder than words, for this courageous venture is already secured, both artistically and financially, at least for the next decade.

It was a group of young artists with strong and fresh blood running through their veins whose determination set this movement in motion; it is the most consistent movement in Vienna ever since the fiery temperament and genius of Hans Makart set the world of art on fire. This movement holds great promise; it might follow in the footsteps of all the other great art movements: The "Vereinigung der XI" in Berlin who exhibit their art in Schulte's art gallery or it might even be a Secession just as in Munich, Paris and other art capitals all over the world. It could be an exodus to the Holy Mountain; one part movement of opposition, one part new creation, an "Anti-Salon" which will – by nature – always be a salon for the rejected.

At the same time, however, these bold, young Austrians are considerate patriots. They want to be neither *frondeurs*[3] nor *Watergeuzen*[4] and even less do they want to wage a guerilla war against the Academy and the *Künstlerhaus*. It is not the urge to rebel against their elders that is driving them forward. They are not out to offend anyone or to celebrate themselves. No, their goal is to elevate the traditional, classical Austrian art to a modern, international level. The artists themselves put their intention into the following words:

---

1. This essay was the first notice that the public received about the formation of the *"V.b.K.Ö"*
2. In the end another address was chosen in the Wienzeile (Friedrichstraße)
3. Seventeenth century member of the faction vying for limiting the king's power during the *Fronde*, a French civil war
4. Sixteenth century Dutch pirates and freedom fighters; from French *Gueux de mer*

Gnawing Sorrow
(detail from second panel of
The Beethoven Frieze), 1902.
Casin on plaster, height: 220 cm.
Secession, Vienna.

The Death of Juliet, 1886.
Black pencil with white highlights,
27.6 x 42.4 cm.
Graphische Sammlung Albertina,
Vienna.

Man's Head Lying Down
(painting from the ceiling of the
Imperial Venetian Theatre), 1886-1888.
Black chalk, white highlights, 28 x 43 cm.
Graphische Sammlung Albertina,
Vienna.

"A band of young artists has, driven by an ideal and an unshakeable faith in Vienna's artistic future, undeterred by any obstacle - founded an association of visual artists for Austria. With the help of several true friends of the arts and supporters who are willing to make sacrifices and disregard material hardship, they want to follow their calling and be artistically active."

Despite their non-confrontational intentions, the *V.b.K.Ö* is still a "warlike" association because they wanted to fight the lack of ideas and the artistic phlegm in today's art scene. This goal is not to be reached by arguing polemically but by aiming for purely artistic ideals and educating the "eye", the art perception of the masses so that they can better understand the living, ever-evolving nature of art. This better alternative will thus become an enemy of everything that was only "good" so far and, naturally, even more hostile towards the "bad".

This task requires immense endurance, for the public has to be broken of it's tolerance for bad art. The "bad" has simply to be made impossible by silencing the demand for it. The necessity for a new renaissance in the arts is evidenced by the presence of quite a few famous names - which are beyond any suspicion of being youthful upstarts - that are joining the ranks of the movement. Grandmaster Rudolf Alt was asked to act as honorary president. Which accusation could there be that is not disproved by his presence? Quite a few academic professors are joining the ranks of the artists: Myslbek, Hellmer, Julian Falat, Hynais. Among our young members are Engelhart and Moll, whose determination is the stuff of legends; Bernatzik, Bacher, Klimt, Krämer, Knüpfer, Mayreder, Ottenfeld, Stöhr, Jettel and Dei have also joined the group.[5]

Artists from all of Europe are sending their regards and cheering their colleagues on; New-Munich and New-Berlin are standing shoulder to shoulder with New-Vienna. Stuck, Marr, Herterich, Dettmann, Kuehl, Dill and many more, even some Parisian masters, have joined the group as "non-residential members". A youth association is international by concept and cannot be anything other than international; youth organizations all over the world share the same goal: to celebrate life to the fullest.

This general, international approval is an important safeguard for the Viennese group. It provides them with contacts beyond Austria, which is highly crucial, since it is getting more and more difficult to organize a Viennese exhibition with a European character. Even during the last international exhibition in the *Künstlerhaus,* the 30,000 guilders that had been granted by the government were not sufficient to purchase foreign artworks. Munich, Berlin and Dresden allow their art galleries to keep up with the development in the world of art und thus give their youth access to a modern artistic education. By contrast, in Vienna the circumstances are getting more difficult; without the Emperor and the Prince of Liechtenstein things would have gotten worse already.

Especially this year's spring exhibition made Vienna's isolated position painfully apparent. Such a lack of inspiration has not been seen in an annual exhibition in a long time. The artists are acting as ·if they were members of a private club; they know each other so well that no one has to say anything new or to contribute anything innovative. We actually know the reason why Vienna's art scene is getting bogged down. We have pointed it out on several occasions: the lure of prestige.

The floor in the *Academy* and the *Künstlerhaus* is littered with the cudgels that have been taken up on the behalf of various causes: this academic chair or that coveted award or a jury decision or yet another important commission. The downside of practicing art competitively and in community with other artists has revealed itself dramatically in the confined space that is the art scene of Vienna.

Allegory of Sculpture, 1889.
Pencil and watercolour, 44 x 30 cm.
Historisches Museum, Vienna.

---

5. Some artists (Myslbek, Delug, Knüpfer) left but others soon joined

GVSTAV·KLIMT·
M·D·C·C·C·L·X·X·X·I·X·

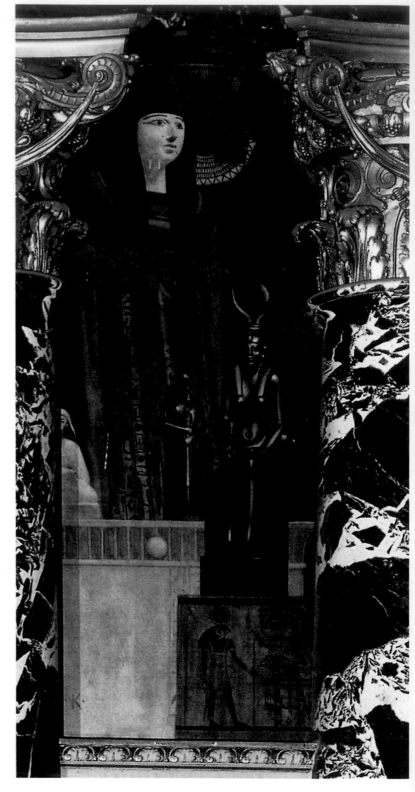

Left: *Greek Art*, 1890-1891.
Oil on plaster, 230 x 80 cm.
Kunsthistorisches Museum, Vienna.

Right: *Egyptian Art II*, 1890-1891.
Oil on plaster, 230 x 80 cm.
Kunsthistorisches Museum, Vienna.

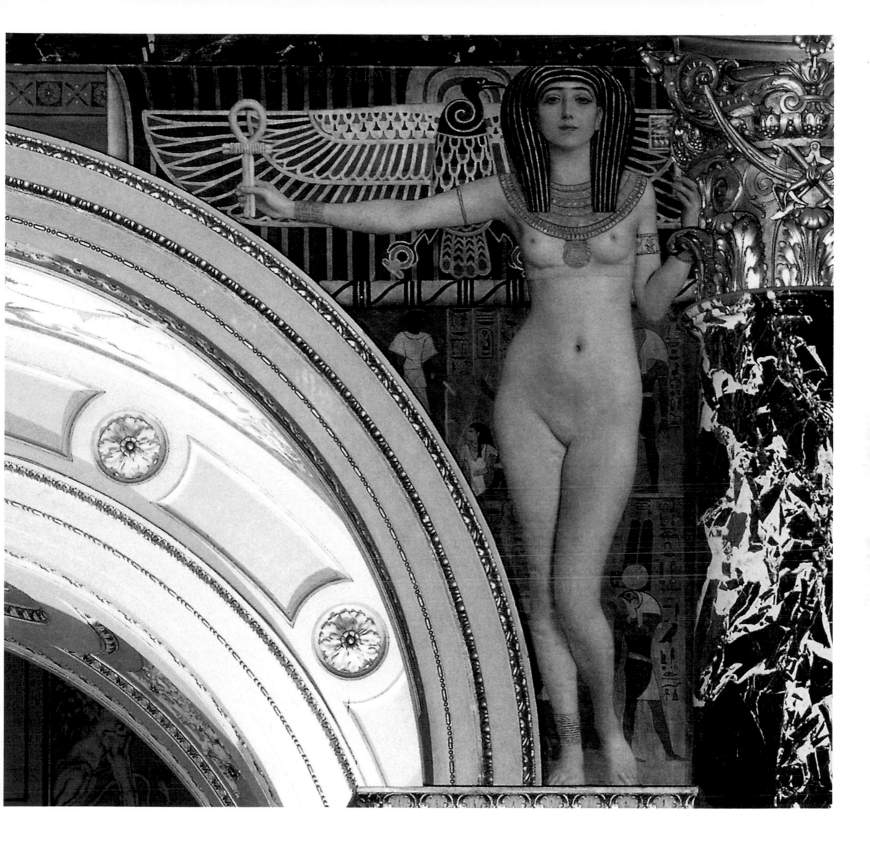

Egyptian Art I
(Young Girl with Horus), 1890-1891.
Oil on plaster, 230 x 230.
Kunsthistorisches Museum, Vienna.

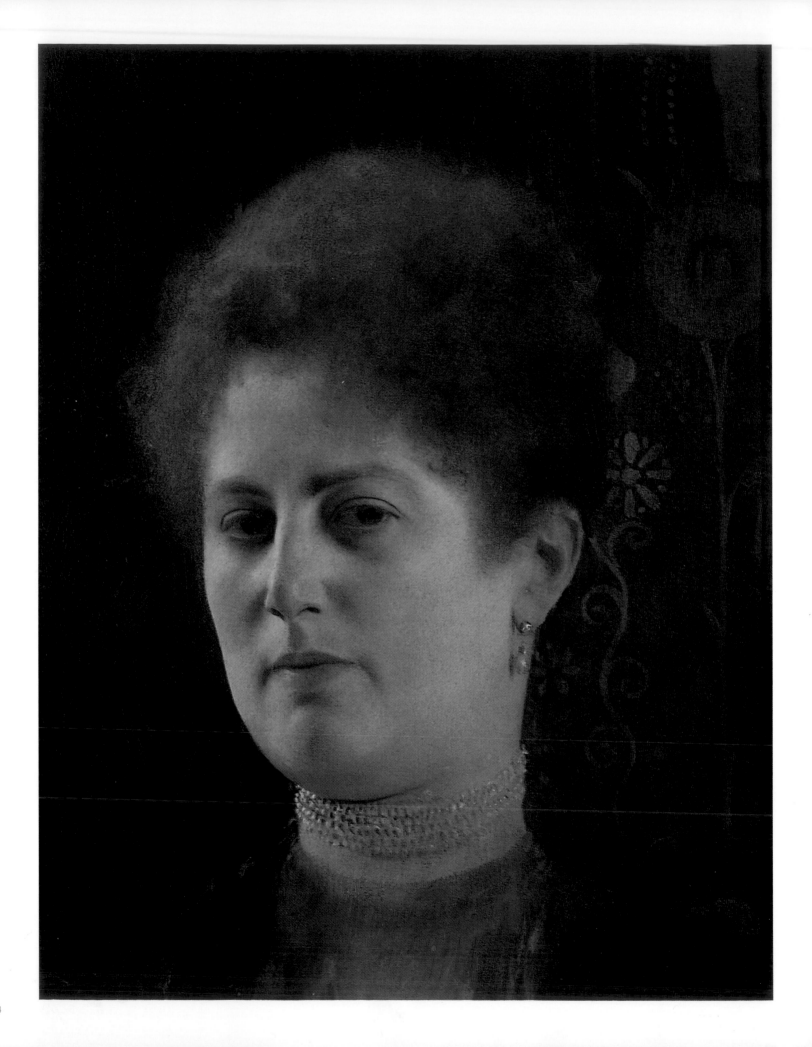

14

So, it is also an act of self-help when these young artists, with their unbreakable spirit, make themselves ready to strike out at the old clutter so that the art scene can finally breathe fresh air again. This new association will make it possible to have healthy competition again.

Some things will be made impossible, such as the atrocity that did not allow someone like Emil Jakob Schindler, two years before his death, at the height of his brilliance, to exhibit the 28 paintings he wished to show to the world but instead allowed him to show only 14 paintings, which were, moreover, displayed apart from each other, completely out of context. If Schindler was still alive today he would surely go to the *Wollzeile* to display his art.

The fire that has been ignited by this movement needs to be maintained, just like fuelling a fireplace; for this very reason the exhibition center is being planned and built. From this new and free house of artists maybe even the Academy can be won over and a modern gallery can be established, a Viennese *Luxembourg*[6]. The whole profit of future exhibitions is going to be invested into such a modern gallery; the gallery will only blossom out of a well-nurtured stem. The new house is going be a focal point and a staging area for the still scattered Austrian forces and even the province will be fed artistically out of this rich larder. There will be "elite-exhibitions" in every city so that even those that have been disinherited of their art appreciation can feel part of a beautiful body; the body of art. There is much blessing to impart. There even shall be art for the people. If, for example, a young law student asks the administration of the gallery for free entry, the request should be considered and a way found to realize the plea, so that the need for art is satisfied. Ultimately we want these young people to, God willing, buy the works from our painting and sculpting progeny.[7]

It is a pleasant phenomenon that this particular movement combines passion with reason. Without dreaming about a utopian future for their art collective and without trumpets or fireworks these young people of the *Vereinigung* have approached the challenge pragmatically. Rich patrons of the art have been admitted into confidence so that the authorities of Vienna and the urban expansion office could see the importance of this project early on. Everything that was needed could be purchased cheaply by those bold men. Not often has the determination of a few prepared the ground for artistic creation. Everyone who supported this project in even the littlest measure deserves the praise of the public. The project has progressed even so far that the construction plan for the new exhibition center should be finished soon. On the plot of land spanning 1200 square metres, that has been granted by the council, a true art palace of 640 square metres with a will rise, surrounded by an aesthetically pleasing recreation area. The building is planned as a public building with a raised ground floor with a skylight and now windows; the outer walls will be artfully decorated with frescos so that Vienna not even gets a center of art but also a structural ornament. The financial means for the execution and maintenance of the project have been secured and now the artists are hoping to be able to open the doors of their new home soon.

"May visionary friends of the arts," the V.b.K.Ö says in their message, "may first and foremost those citizens of Vienna who are enthusiastic about art, honour our endeavours and support them as best they can. May patrons and artists strive together to make Vienna into what it is destined to be: Vienna, City of Art. (27 March 1897)."

---

6. Refers to the Musée des artistes vivants, established in the Palais du Luxembourg in Paris between 1818 and 1937 to house the French state's collection of contemporary art.

7. The Künstlerhaus rejected such requests

Portrait of a Woman
(possibly Mrs. Heymann), c. 1894.
Oil on wood, 39 x 23 cm.
Kunsthistorisches Museum, Vienna.

After the Rain, 1899.
Oil on canvas, 80 x 40 cm.
Österreichische Galerie Belvedere,
Vienna.

Water Sprites (Silver Fish), 1899.
Oil on canvas, 82 x 52 cm.
Kunstsammlung Bank Austria AG,
Vienna.

His Life

Beautiful, sensuous, and, above all, erotic, Gustav Klimt's paintings speak of a world of opulence and leisure, which seems eons away from the harsh, post-modern environment we live in now. The subjects he treats – allegories, portraits, landscapes and erotic figures – contain virtually no reference to external events, but strive rather to create a world where beauty, above everything else, is dominant.

His use of colour and pattern, profoundly influenced by the art of Japan, ancient Egypt, and Byzantine Ravenna, the flat, two-dimensional perspective of his paintings, and the frequently stylized quality of his images form an œuvre imbued with a profound sensuality and one where the figure of woman, above all, reigns supreme.

Beginnings

Klimt's very first works brought him success at an unusually early age. He came from a poor family where his father, a goldsmith and engraver, could scarcely support his wife and family of seven children. Gustav, born in 1862, obtained a state grant to study at the Kunstgewerbeschule (the Vienna School of Art) at the age of fourteen. His talents as a draughtsman and painter were quickly noticed, and in 1879 he formed the Künstlerkompagnie (Artists' Company) with his brother Ernst and another student, Franz Matsch.

The latter part of the nineteenth century was a period of great architectural activity in Vienna. In 1857, the Emperor Franz Joseph had ordered the destruction of the fortifications that had surrounded the medieval city centre. The Ringstrasse was the result, a budding new district with magnificent buildings and beautiful parks, all paid for by public expenses. This meant therefore, that the young Klimt and his partners had ample opportunities to show their talents and they received early commissions to contribute to the decorations for the pageant organized to celebrate the silver wedding of the Emperor Franz Joseph and the Empress Elisabeth. In the following year, they were commissioned to produce a ceiling painting for the thermal baths in Carlsbad. Other public commissions soon followed.

When one examines his early works, such as *Fable* (p. 65), *Idyll* (p. 66), or indeed one of Klimt's earliest drawings, *Male Nude Walking Facing Right*, it is clear that he is a painter of great skill and promise, but remains entirely within the accepted contemporary norms in his depiction of academic and allegorical subjects. The women depicted in *Fable* and *Idyll* are plump, adroitly draped in plain clothing, their hair smoothly pulled back behind the neck. Neither would look out of place in the eighteenth or even seventeenth century. Their sensuality is matronly, motherly, their nudity decorous rather than exciting.

In the past, pubic hair had – if this part of the body was revealed at all – traditionally been glossed over into a smooth and non-threatening 'v' reminiscent of modern-day children's dolls. Many early medieval or Renaissance paintings which had shown even the suggestion of male or

Tree of Life (detail), c.1905-1909.
Museum für Angewandte Kunst,
Vienna.

Two Girls with Oleander, 1890.
Oil on canvas, 55 x 128.5 cm,
Wadsworth Atheneum, Hartford
(Connecticut).

female genitalia had suffered the absurd addition of a floating fig leaf painted in by later, more prudish, types. But even as early as 1896, Klimt had begun to be more explicit in the way he chose to depict the human figure.

There is, for example, an interesting difference between the final drawing for *Sculpture* (p. 34) and the painting itself. In the drawing we already see the trademark loose, wild, dark hair and the faintest traces of pubic hair. The woman gazes directly at the viewer, standing as if caught naked in her bedroom doorway, summoning the viewer to caress her. The painting, by contrast, has reverted to a more traditional style: gone is the frontal stance, with the reappearance of the classical sculptural pose. Up goes the hair and the pubic hair disappears.

Secession

These early commissions established Klimt as a successful and prominent artist. Following the death of his father and brother Ernst in 1892, there seems to have been a distinct cooling-off in the working relationship between Klimt and Matsch as Klimt began to explore more adventurous subjects.

In 1894, Matsch moved out of their shared studio, and in 1897 Klimt, together with his closest friends, resigned from the Künstlerhausgenossenschaft (the Cooperative Society of Austrian Artists) to form a new movement known as the Secession, of which he was immediately elected president.

Woman near the Fire, 1897-1898.
Oil on canvas, 41 x 66 cm.
Österreichische Galerie Belvedere,
Vienna.

The Golden Knight (Life is a Fight),
1903. Oil, tempera and gold on canvas,
103.5 x 103.7 cm.
Aichi Prefectural Museum of Art,
Nagoya, Japan.

*The Beethoven Frieze: Suffering
Humanity, Ambition, Compassion and
the Knight in Shining Armor*
(left panel, detail), 1902.
Casein on plaster, height: 220 cm.
Secession, Vienna.

The Beethoven Frieze: The Gorgons
(central panel, detail), 1902.
Casein on plaster, height: 220 cm.
Secession, Vienna.

The Secession was a great success, holding both a first and a second exhibition in 1898. The movement made enough money to commission their very own building, designed for them by the architect Joseph Maria Olbrich. Above the entrance was their motto: "To each age its art, to art its freedom". The Secession not only came to represent the best of Austrian art, but was also successful in the bringing together of Viennese-French Impressionist and Belgian Naturalist works, which had never before been seen by the Austrian public.

Klimt was undoubtedly the central figure in this young and dynamic movement, but his success as a modern artist went hand in hand with the loss of his status as an accepted and established painter.

As he moved away from his traditional beginnings, he soon found himself at the centre of a series of scandals, which were to change his entire career.

Scandal

In 1894, Klimt and Matsch had received a commission to produce a series of paintings for the University of Vienna. The subjects Klimt was assigned were philosophy, medicine, and jurisprudence. The nature of the commission can easily be imagined: the university would be expecting a series of dignified, formal paintings in classical style depicting the wisdom of

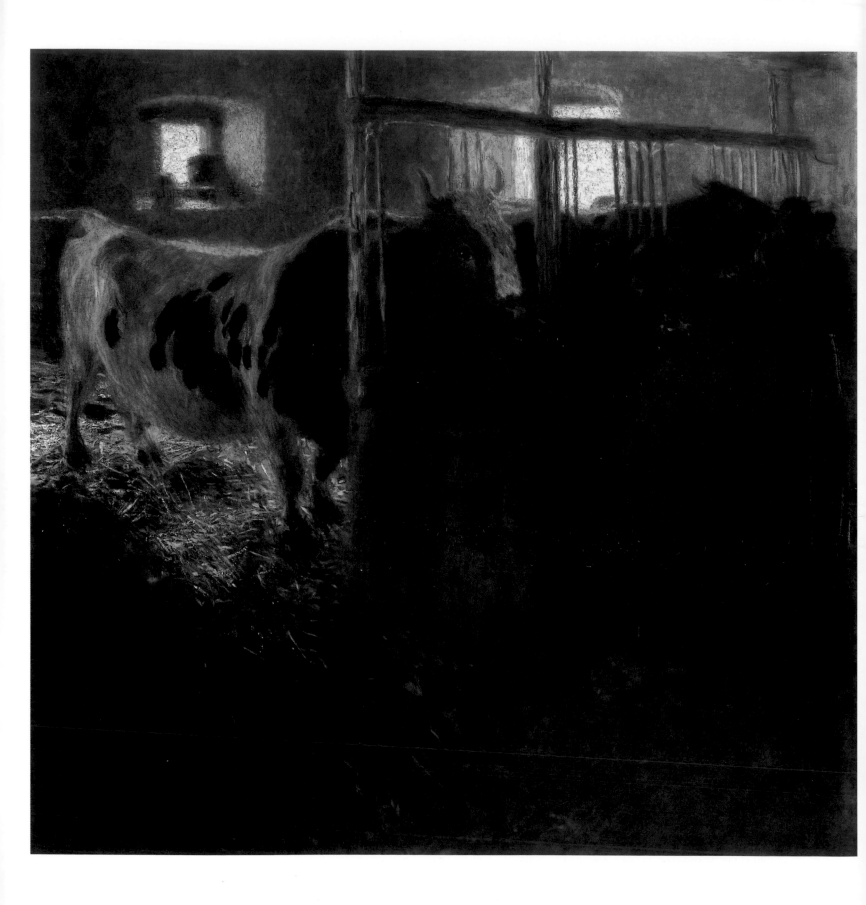

philosophers, the healing virtues of medicine, and doubtless a statuesque blindfolded female figure holding a pair of scales and representing justice.

What they got, several years and much hard work later, caused such a scandal that Klimt eventually repaid the advances he had received and took the paintings back.

Despite the fact that on its first showing in Paris at the World Fair in 1900 *Philosophy* won him the gold medal, the Viennese were not of the same opinion as the French as to the painting's merits.

The first appearance of the unfinished *Medicine* (p. 133) in the following year caused even greater controversy. It is difficult to fathom precisely what Klimt meant to say about medicine in this painting.

The vision is chaotic, almost hellish. Its skulls, wrinkled elderly figures and mass of human bodies speak of human suffering, not of its cure. The viewer's eyes are drawn inevitably to the two striking female figures at the bottom and top left of the painting. Clearly the figure at the bottom represents Medicine itself as the traditional symbol of the serpent suggests, but rather this art nouveau woman, adorned in gold, looks more like a priestess likely to sacrifice a sick person than to heal them. The naked woman at the top of the picture is remarkable for the dynamic abandonment of her pose. Our eyes are inevitably drawn to the woman's groin as she flings out her arms in a parody of crucifixion.

The sketch for the figure shows very clearly how bold and excellent a craftsman Klimt was: the heavy line and subtle shading lead our eyes firmly to the woman's pubic hair. Interestingly though, in the sketch the woman looks as if she may have posed lying down or leaning against something, whereas in the painting she is standing precariously unsupported, as if about to fall.

Both of these, and the other female figures around them, represent a complete departure from the rotund, comfortable women of the traditional nineteenth-century academic style. Klimt's women are long-haired, slender, lithe, and possess a sexual awareness that is both alluring and almost threatening in its directness.

Klimt's contemporary, Berta Zuckerkandl, makes the following comment in her memoirs: "Klimt had created from Viennese women an ideal female type: modern, with a boyish figure."

They had a mysterious fascination; although the word 'vamp' was still unknown he drew women with the allure of a Greta Garbo or a Marlene Dietrich long before they actually existed." (*Ich erlebte fünfzig Jahre Weltgeschichte* [I Witnessed Fifty Years of World History], Stockholm 1939.) Looking at his 1909 portrait *Woman with a Hat and Feather Boa* (p. 149) it is easy to see the truth of this statement. The woman's face, half-hidden by feathers and a hat, looks not unlike a dark-haired version of Marilyn Monroe. The seductively half-closed eyes certainly echo many Monroe poses.

The Secession's fourteenth exhibition in 1902 led to yet another scandal. The exhibition centred on Max Klinger's statue of Beethoven. Klimt had decided to contribute a frieze. The detail shown on the inside of the next page depicts *Lasciviousness, Wantonness* and *Intemperance* (p. 28), three allegorical figures designed to occupy part of the central wall of the room where Klinger's statue was to be exhibited. Again, Klimt's reason for choosing precisely these subjects for a tribute to Beethoven remains obscure, but they contain the seeds of many later works, most notably the trademark use of exotically patterned textiles to form not so much a backdrop to the human figures, but to create a composition of which pattern and human figure are equal parts.

In the figure of Lasciviousness, shown top left, Klimt uses the woman's hair both to hide her sex and to draw attention to it. The superb figure of Intemperance resembles not so much a woman

Cow Shed, 1899.
Oil on canvas, 75 x 76.5 cm.
Lentos Kunstmuseum Linz, Linz.

The Beethoven Frieze
(central panel, detail), 1902.
Casein on plaster, height: 220 cm.
Secession, Vienna.

Final drawing for *Nuda Veritas*, 1898.
Black chalk, pencil,
Indian ink, 41 x 10 cm.
Historiches Museum, Vienna.

Jurisprudence, 1907.
Oil on canvas, 430 x 300 cm.
Burnt in 1945 at Immendorf Castle.

as an oriental pasha, a man whose corpulence has reached such an extent that his chest has expanded to form female breasts.

Conservative Viennese society was once again profoundly shocked by these images, much in the same way that modern-day exhibition-goers are shocked by a Damien Hirst. Klimt's contemporary Felix Salten relates: "Suddenly an exclamation came from the centre of the room: 'Hideous!' An aristocrat, a patron and collector, whom the Secession had let in today together with other close friends, had lost his temper at the sight of the Klimt frescoes. He shouted the word in a high, shrill, sharp voice... he threw it up the walls like a stone.:'Hideous!'"

Klimt's only response to this, as he worked away on the scaffolding above, was an amused glance in the direction of the departed man. This calm response perhaps best typifies Klimt's reaction to the scandals he caused.

Although the faculty paintings ensured that Klimt swiftly lost the patronage of the Emperor and other establishment figures, he was fortunate enough to be able to earn an extremely comfortable living from painting portraits and thus did not have to worry about this loss. Three times, however, he was refused a professorship of the Academy. Only in 1917 was he offered the small consolation of being made an honorary member.

Fin de Siècle Vienna

It must be remembered that despite their tastes for balls, the opera, theatre and music, the Viennese upper classes were extremely conservative in their tastes. A combination of strict Roman Catholicism and rigid social morals kept them buttoned up, at least on the surface. And whilst people were only too happy to indulge in all sorts of sensual pleasures that were sanctioned by society – the waltz, for example – they did not appreciate having openly erotic, ugly or sexual subjects thrust before them, a double standard which speaks volumes about fin de siècle morality.

The Vienna into which Klimt was born was a city perched uncomfortably on the cusp of two eras. Then, it was still the capital of a far-reaching empire of over fifty million inhabitants, ruled by the Emperor Franz Joseph.

However, by the time of Klimt's death in 1918, the Habsburg Empire itself had only seven months left to live. Austria then became a tiny nation state of seven million inhabitants, three million of whom were concentrated around Vienna. Twenty years later it was absorbed by Nazi Germany under the leadership of Adolf Hitler, himself, ironically, born on Austrian soil.

The period of decline had begun even before Klimt was born. Military defeats across the Empire sounded warning bells for future stability, whilst Vienna was filling up with Czechs, gypsies, Hungarians, Poles, Jews, and Romanians – immigrants from the poorest parts of the Empire, all in search of work, often living in appalling conditions. The wealthy Viennese, however, chose not to acknowledge these signals of future trouble but rather to ignore the outside world and immerse themselves in a whirl of pleasurable activities.

This was a period of great musicians – Brahms, Bruckner, Strauss the younger, Schönberg, Mahler and, of course, Franz Lehár, creator of the light operettas so beloved of the Viennese. It was also the era of Sigmund Freud, Alfred Adler, Arthur Schnitzler, and amidst all this, Klimt.

Lovers and Friends

One of the most tantalising facts about a man so well-known in times comparatively recent to our own is that almost nothing concrete is known about Klimt's personal life, a fact largely due to his own reticence on the subject. Whilst the facts of his artistic career are well-charted, knowledge of

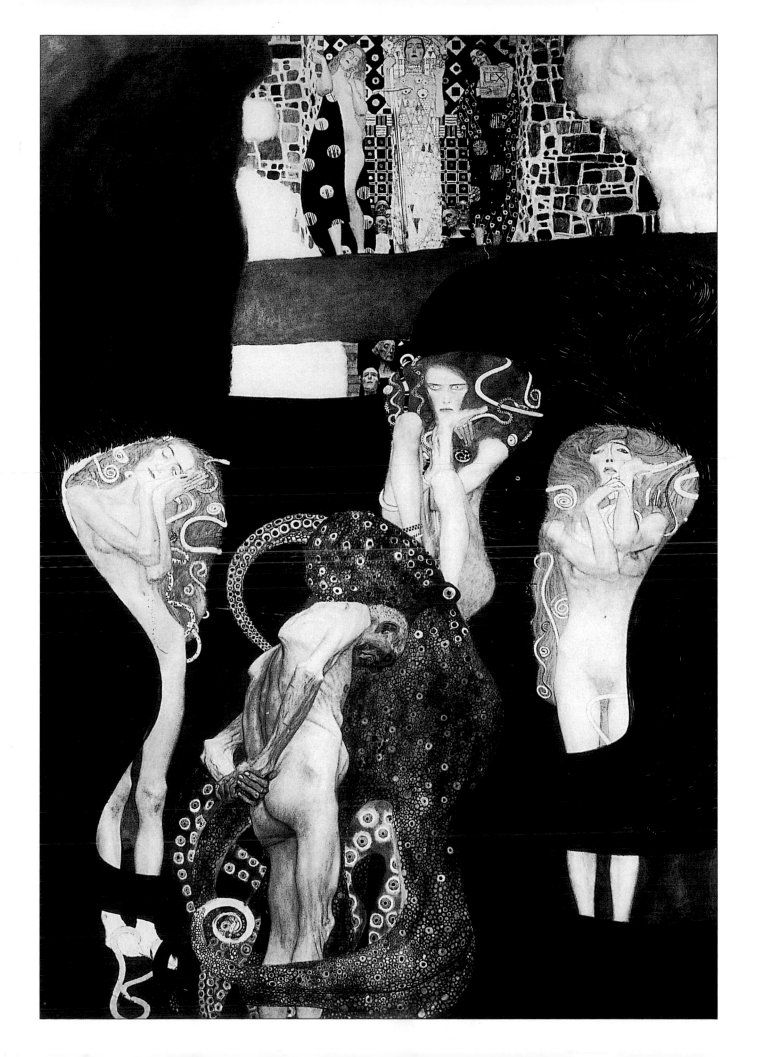

Music, 1901. Lithograph.

Marie Moll, 1902-1903.
Pencil, 45.2 x 31.4 cm.
Kunsthistorisches Museum, Vienna.

Fairy Tale, 1884.
Black pencil and ink wash,
63.9 x 34.3 cm.
Kunsthistorisches Museum, Vienna.

Final drawing for the allegory of
Sculpture, 1902-1903.
Black pencil, graphite pencil lead,
wash and gold, 41.8 x 32.3 cm.
Historisches Museum, Vienna.

SCVLPTVR·

GVSTAV·KLIMT·
MDCCCIVC·

Flowing Water, 1898.
Oil on canvas, 52 x 65 cm.
Private collection.

his private life depends entirely on hearsay. On the one hand, he is depicted as a ladies' man, built like a peasant, strong as an ox, sleeping with countless women, including all of his models. On the other hand, he is seen as a hypochondriac and a confirmed bachelor with a balanced lifestyle, living with his mother and sisters while keeping a studio in the suburbs to which he went to work regularly every day:

> Klimt's daily routines were very bourgeois. He was so engrossed in them that any divergence from his normal course was a horror to him; going anywhere was a major event, and a big trip was only conceivable if his friends did all the shopping for him beforehand, down to the smallest detail.
>
> (Hans Tietze, *Gustav Klimts Persönlichkeit nach Mitteilungen seiner Freunde* [Gustav Klimt's Personality According to Messages from His Friends], 1919).

Klimt never married, but had a long relationship with Emilie Flöge, the sister of his brother Ernst's wife. In 1891, Ernst had married Helene Flöge, one of two sisters who ran a fashion house in Vienna. The marriage only lasted fifteen months, but through Helene, Gustav met Emilie. From around 1897 onwards, he spent almost every summer on the Attersee with the Flöge family, periods of peace and tranquillity, which produced the landscape paintings constituting almost a quarter of his entire œuvre.

The exact nature of Klimt's relationship with Emilie Flöge remains unknown. They never lived together, and although it was Emilie whom Klimt requested on his death bed, there has always been a great deal of speculation as to whether they were actually lovers.

Klimt corresponded extensively both with Emilie and with Marie (Mizzi) Zimmerman, who was the mother of two of his three illegitimate children. He writes to Marie with great affection and in

Death's Procession, 1903.
Burnt in 1945 at Immendorf Castle.

Roses in Trees, 1904.
Oil on canvas, 110 x 110 cm.
Musée d'Orsay, Paris.

Pear Tree, 1903.
Oil and casein on canvas,
101 x 101 cm.
Harvard University Art Museums,
Cambridge, Massachusetts.

detail about his work and daily life, whilst to Emilie he appears to write merely in order to communicate information concerning travel arrangements and other such neutral details.

But who is to tell where the truth ultimately lies? It is perfectly possible that more personal correspondence between Klimt and Emilie did exist, but was subsequently destroyed.

His 1902 portrait of Emilie (p. 113) shows an attractive young woman wearing one of her own dresses, many of which Klimt designed for her fashion house, as well as jewellery and textiles. It's a remarkably subdued painting, with just a subtle, tantalising hint of sensuality in the light patch of skin just above the bodice, suggesting the hidden breast beneath. How different from the 1903 painting *Hope I* (p. 117), which depicts a naked and heavily pregnant woman, Herma, one of Klimt's favourite models.

The story goes that one day Herma, whom Klimt apparently described as having a backside more beautiful and more intelligent than the faces of many other models, failed to turn up for work. Klimt, who took very good care of his models, began to worry and finally sent someone to find out if she was ill. Upon hearing that she was not ill but pregnant, Klimt insisted that she came to work anyway. She then became the model for *Hope I*.

This fragile, slender woman looking calmly out at the viewer is anything but maternal. Her figure, apart from her distended stomach, is still that of a young woman, thin to the point of skinniness. Her hair is crowned with flowers as if she were a bride. Depending on one's point of view, her direct gaze and unashamed nakedness shown in profile for maximum effect, are either pointing out the obvious consequences of sex, or inviting a still-sexual response to her body.

The later *Hope II* (p. 138), painted in 1907-1908, has a far more maternal feel. The woman's breasts are full and large-nippled, her head bowed in a peaceful, almost Madonna-like pose. She is enclosed by a fabric that follows an abruptly straight line down her back as if she were actually sitting on a straight-backed chair being carried by the figures underneath her. The last great hope of humankind, transported on the backs of other women.

When Klimt died, there were no fewer than fourteen claims that he was the father of an illegitimate child, only three of which were legally upheld – two by Marie Zimmerman and one by Maria Ucicky. (The child was named Gustav after his father and later went on to become a film director). It is generally assumed that he slept with most of his models.

He was certainly known to be very generous towards them. Who knows whether the pregnancies depicted in his paintings had any connection with the painter himself? If they did, Herma's gaze in *Hope I* takes on an entirely new meaning: a look of reproach? Or one of irony?

Drawings and Sketches

In his studio, Klimt kept girls available to him at all times, waiting for him in a room next door in case he decided to paint them. Franz Servaes, a contemporary art critic, observed: "Here he was surrounded by mysterious, naked female creatures, who, while he stood silent in front of his easel, strolled around his studio, stretching themselves, lazing around and enjoying the day – always ready for the command of the master obediently to stand still whenever he caught sight of a pose or a movement that appealed to his sense of beauty and that he would then capture in a rapid drawing."

Klimt made sketches for virtually everything he did. Sometimes there were over a hundred drawings for one painting, each showing a different detail – a piece of clothing or jewellery, or a simple gesture. They would lie about his studio in heaps, where his adored cats, it is said, had a habit of destroying them.

Young Girl with a Blue Veil,
1902-1903.
Oil on canvas, 67 x 55 cm.
Private collection.

Orchard, 1905-1906.
Oil on canvas, 98.7 x 99.4 cm.
The Carnegie Museum of Art,
Pittsburgh.

Garden Landscape, 1906.
Oil on canvas, 110 x 110 cm.
Private collection.

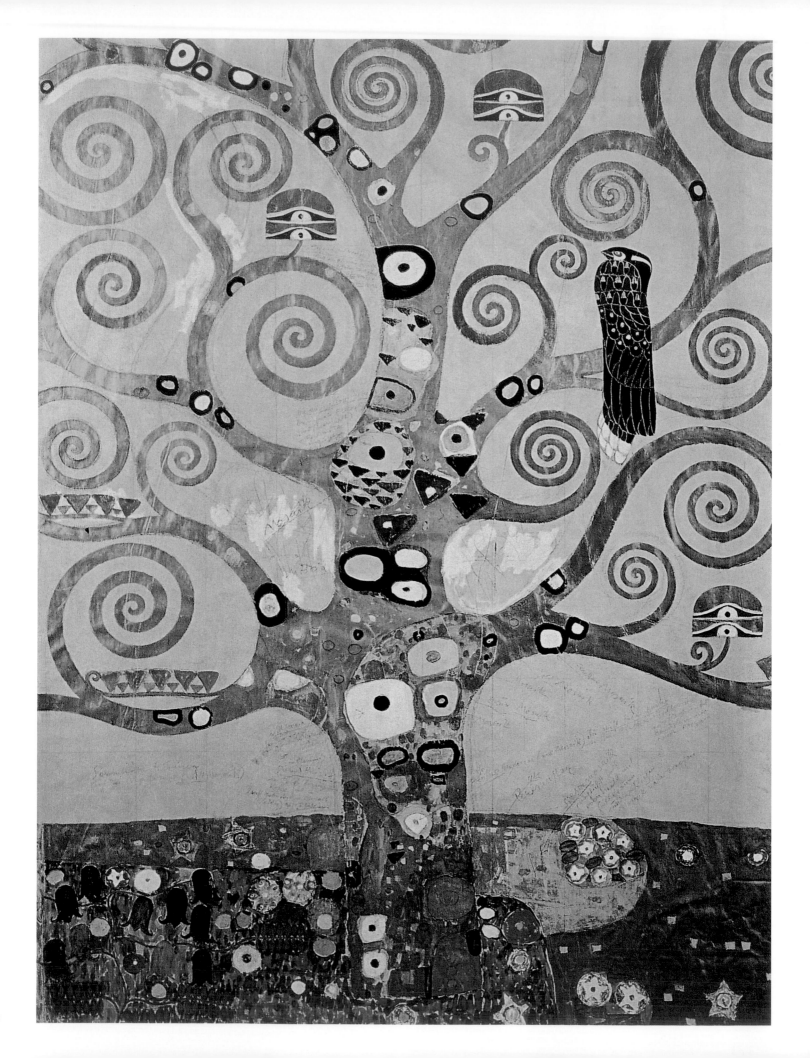

Unfortunately, however, the bulk of his sketchbooks were destroyed not by cats but by a fire in Emilie Flöge's apartment. Only three of the books survived. The drawings which have survived, however, provide a fascinating insight into Klimt's artistic and personal preoccupations: whereas in his paintings nudity and sexuality are covered, almost imprisoned by ornament and textile to be partially and tantalisingly revealed, in his drawings eroticism is open and undisguised.

Even during his lifetime, his drawings were regarded by some critics as the best work of his entire life's work, but they would not have been widely seen. Luckily for him, unlike Schiele, who earned his living from his drawings, Klimt's income was derived entirely from his painting. Drawing for him was either a necessary preparatory process or a form of relaxation, a way of expressing himself spontaneously free from the constraints and detail of oil.

Klimt's drawings not only reveal his mastery of illustrating, they also show an erotic obsession and a sexual freedom quite at odds with the covered-up, repressed society in which he moved. In these drawings there is no visual, temporal, or spatial context, just the women themselves, who were presumably, as earlier described, wandering around his studio in a state of undress. He draws them only in outline, omitting any internal modeling or shading of their bodies and almost always drawing attention to their genitalia or breasts by using perspective, foreshortening, distortion or other formal techniques.

A wonderful example of how a couple of pencil strokes can be used to devastatingly erotic effect is the 1905-1906 drawing *Friends Embracing*, in which a tiny circle of darkness draws the viewer's gaze automatically between the woman's legs and her buttocks.

The women are frequently depicted masturbating, absorbed in their own sensual pleasures, eyes closed, face slightly averted. How very at ease these women must have felt with Klimt to allow him to portray them in this way!

Languorous, feline, and utterly absorbed, they masturbate delicately, fingers poised above the clitoris, still fully or partially clothed, eyes closed in the imaginary heat of a summer's afternoon.

Sometimes Klimt draws in great detail, sometimes it is the overall pose that clearly interests him. Men rarely make an appearance in these drawings, and when they do they are almost uniquely depicted with their back to the viewer. In general, apart from academic studies at art school, men are peripheral figures in Klimt's paintings. Their faces are rarely shown, and they seem to exist either as voyeurs or simply as the physical partner to a sexual act, of which the woman is the main point of interest for the viewer. What is extraordinary in Klimt's work is that, while expressing his clear admiration for women's beauty, when he shows men and women together he articulates a kind of remoteness, a gulf between the sexes.

In his painting *The Kiss* (p. 141), the man's face cannot be seen. He holds the woman up, his hands clasped round her face in a gesture of great tenderness, yet her face is turned away from his embrace: he is offered only her cheek to kiss, and her hand looks almost as if she were trying to pull his away. Auguste Rodin's earlier sculpture *The Kiss*, by contrast, shows both lovers fully engaged in their embrace. It is a tender, romantic and sensual moment equally involving both partners. One could assuredly interpret this lack of direct contact in Klimt's painting in other terms — her face is turned towards us so that we can admire its peaceful beauty, for example — but another sketch of 1903-1904 presents a series of images that underline the first interpretation: the figures are seated in a pose similar to that of the lovers in Rodin's sculpture. The man, however, seems unable to make any physical contact with the woman, desperately though he tries. He clasps her to him, leans over her, and finally leans on top of her in an attitude of despair. Are we to infer from this a vision of the world in which men desperately seek love

Tree of Life, c.1905-1909.
195 x 102 cm.
Museum für Angewandte Kunst,
Vienna.

Waiting, c.1905-1909.
Cardboard for the *Stoclet Frieze*,
193.5 x 115 cm.
Österreichisches Museum, Vienna.

Accomplishment, c.1905-1909.
Cardboard for the *Stoclet Frieze*,
194.6 x 120.3 cm.
Österreichisches Museum, Vienna.

from women who, though appearing open to this contact, actually possess a quiet, independent world quite inaccessible to men?

One of Klimt's amorous liaisons might suggest so. Alma Mahler-Werfel (then Schindler) knew Klimt when she was a young girl of seventeen and claims that he was in love with her. She was not a modest diarist by any means, but there is no reason to doubt the truth of the affair, especially in the light of a later letter of apology written by Klimt to her stepfather, Carl Moll. Alma later made something of a career out of having relationships with artists: she was married three times, first to Gustav Mahler, then to the architect Walter Gropius, then finally to the Prague poet Franz Werfel, with a wild love affair with Oskar Kokoschka thrown in for good measure in between.

Of her youthful infatuation with Klimt she writes: "He was the most gifted of them all, thirty-five years of age, at the zenith of his powers, beautiful in every sense of the word and already famous. His beauty and my youthful freshness, his genius, my talents, the profound life-melody we shared touched the same chords in us both. I was ridiculously ignorant of all things passionate – and he felt and found me everywhere… He was bound by a hundred chains: women, children, even sisters who fought over him. But he still followed me…"

Society Portraits

The freedom of Klimt's drawings stands in marked contrast with the portraits of society women he produced between 1903 and around 1913 where the women in his drawings are unconstrained either by clothes or by social conventions. He depicts Fritza Riedler and Adele Bloch-Bauer awash in a sea of pattern and ornament. Their faces stand out, serious and composed, before blocks of pattern or colour strategically placed behind their heads to emphasize their features to the maximum.

Girlfriends, 1905.
Black chalk, 45 x 31 cm.
Historisches Museum, Vienna.

Pine Forest II, 1901.
Oil on canvas, 91.5 x 89 cm.
Private collection.

Pond at Kammer Castle on the
Attersee, 1909.
Oil on canvas, 110 x 110 cm.
Private collection.

The Park, 1909-1910.
Oil on canvas, 110.5 x 110.5 cm.
The Museum of Modern Art,
New York.

Lying Lovers, 1908.
Black chalk, 35 x 55 cm.
Historisches Museum, Vienna.

Their bodies are submerged in swathes of textile patterns merging with the background so that the face appears isolated, fragile, alone.

The *Portrait of Margaret Stonborough-Wittgenstein* (p. 125) is notable as one of the few which is not dominated by pattern, and is a clear tribute to the work of Whistler, whom Klimt greatly admired. There is also something particularly striking in the gaze and stance of the young Maria Primavesi: she stands, hand on hip, legs apart, the age-old combination of innocence and provocation. These are remarkably delicate portraits.

Each face betrays so much about the sitter – a calmness, or an awkwardness, and in Adele Bloch-Bauer's (p. 137, 161), the only one of these women known also to have been Klimt's lover, it is difficult not to read into her face a desire to pose as luxuriously as Klimt's models did, especially in the 1912 portrait, where her open lips, her gaze, and her direct stance suggest a certain sexual readiness in stark contrast to the upright behaviour which would undoubtedly have been expected of her.

Pattern and Nudity

In Klimt's paintings from the last ten years of his life, pattern, textile and ornament are used to highly erotic effect, emphasizing the nakedness of the body rather than covering it up. It is as if the women he depicts are imprisoned by the textiles and ornaments, an impression heightened by the artist's heavy use of gold (Klimt had visited Ravenna in 1903, where he had greatly admired the famous Byzantine mosaics).

In *Judith II* (p. 150) the clothes seem barely able to contain the energetic nudity of the avenging woman, and in *The Bride* (p. 190) textiles are used as a way of isolating shapes and body parts to create a highly erotic effect.

Pregnant Nude, Standing, Left Profile, study for *Hope II*, 1907.
Black chalk, 49 x 31 cm.
Historisches Museum, Vienna.

Garden and Summit of a Hill, 1916.
Oil on canvas, 110 x 110 cm.
Kunsthaus Zug, Switzerland.

Forest in a Slope Mountain at Unterach on the Attersee, 1917.
Oil on canvas, 110 x 110 cm.
Private collection.

Heads and torsos become fragmented, detached from their bodies. The figure on the far left of the painting almost resembles Man Ray's photograph of a woman's back as a cello, and the figure to the far right of the canvas has her head totally obscured, leaving her breasts exposed while the lower part of her body is covered by a sexy, see-through skirt leaving her legs open and genitals clearly visible.

The fact that the provocatively naked body exists beneath these skimpy clothes might even suggest, as some of Klimt's preparatory drawings imply, that in other paintings he actually drew the naked body first, then covered it with textiles and pattern. This, at least, is the impression one has when looking at paintings such as *Virgin* (p. 169) in which the young girl, depicted asleep, is lying flat on her back in a pose at once innocent and sexually exposed. The clothes look as if they have been thrown on top of her as if to hide her sexual dreams, represented by the mass of semi-naked, presumably more knowing women underneath her.

Klimt's Legacy

During his entire lifetime, Klimt made only one statement about himself and his art: "I am certain that there is nothing exceptional about me as a person. I am simply a painter who paints every day from morning till night. … I'm not much good at speaking and writing, especially when I have to discuss myself or my work. Just the idea of having to write a simple letter fills me with anguish. I am very much afraid that you will have to do without a portrait of me, either painted or in words, but that is no great loss. Whoever seeks to know me better, that is to say as an artist — and that's the only thing worth knowing — should study my paintings and try to glean from them who I am and what I want."

Just how exceptional Gustav Klimt was is perhaps reflected in the fact that he had no predecessors and no real followers. He admired Rodin and Whistler without slavishly copying them, and was admired in turn by the younger Viennese painters Egon Schiele and Oskar Kokoschka, both of whom were greatly influenced by Klimt. But whereas Klimt belongs to that transitional period at end of the nineteenth century, Schiele and Kokoschka represent the beginnings of that quintessentially early twentieth-century movement, expressionism.

Schiele, like Klimt, produced many drawings of nudes, but where Klimt's drawings were peaceful, dreamy and delicate, Schiele reflected a tortured and neurotic psyche. He drew himself endlessly — an emaciated, troubled figure — and his drawings of female nudes manage to render the women simultaneously sexually attractive and repulsive.

On January 11, 1918, Klimt suffered a stroke that left him partially paralyzed on one side. Although he seemed to be recovering, he died a month later. After his death, opinion was still divided as to his merits as an artist.

Hans Tietze, a friend of Klimt and author of the first monograph on the artist, sums up his importance:

> "Klimt took Viennese painting…out of the isolation in which it was languishing and back again into the wide world…At the turn of the century he, more than anyone else, guaranteed the artistic individuality of Vienna."

Klimt, it has been said, could not have existed anywhere but in Vienna. So totally have the images created by him come to represent the Austrian capital at that time that it could indeed be argued that Vienna could not have entered into the twentieth century without the bold vision and artistic individuality of Klimt.

Garden in Bloom, 1905.
Oil on canvas, 110 x 110 cm.
Private collection.

Squatting Woman, 1919.
Graphite, black pencil and ink wash,
54.9 x 34.8 cm.
Museum der Stadt Wien, Vienna.

Woman Seated with Open Thighs,
1916.
Graphite, white highlights, red pencil,
57 x 38 cm.
Private collection.

Leda, 1917 (destroyed).
Oil on canvas, 99 x 99 cm.

Portrait of a Woman, 1917-1918.
Oil on canvas, 67 x 56 cm.
Lentos Kunstmuseum Linz, Linz.

Waiting (detail) 1905-1909.
Cardboard for the *Stoclet Frieze,*
193.5 x 115cm.
Osterreichisches Museum, Vienna

His Work

Fable	65	Sunflower Garden	129
The Idyll	66	Portrait of Fritza Riedler	130
The Theatre of Taormina	69	Medicine	133
Female Nude Lying Down	70	Hygieia	134
Auditorium of the Old Burgtheater	73	Portrait of Adele Bloch-Bauer I	137
Portrait of Joseph Pembaur	74	Hope II	138
Ancient Greek Art I	77	The Kiss	141
The Love	78	The Kiss (Detail)	142
Music I	81	Danaë	145
Final Drawing for Allegory of Tragedy	82	Kammer Castle on the Attersee I	146
Fish Blood	85	Woman in Hat with Feather Boa	149
Compositional Project for Medicine	86	Judith II	150
Pallas Athena	89	The Black Feather Hat	153
Portrait of Sonja Knips	90	Life and Death	154
Exhibition Wallpaper for Secession I	93	Garden Crucifix	157
Nuda Veritas	94	Farmhouse in Upper Austria	158
Nuda Veritas (Detail)	97	Portrait of Adele Bloch-Bauer II	161
Schubert at Piano	98	Ria Munk on her Death Bed	162
Two Lovers	101	Portrait of Mäda Primavesi	165
Island on the Attersee	102	Portrait of Eugenia Primavesi	166
Goldfish	105	Virgin	169
Judith I	106	Malcesine on Lake Garda	170
Portrait of Gertha Felsovanyi	109	Portrait of Elisabeth Bachofen-Echt	173
The Beethoven Frieze: Ambition, Compassion and the Knight in Shining Armor (Detail)	110	Houses at Unterach on the Attersee	174
Portrait of Emilie Flöge	113	Portrait of Friederike Maria Beer	177
Forest of Beech Trees I	114	Path of Garden and Hens	178
Hope I	117	The Church at Unterach on the Attersee	181
Water Snakes I	118	Girlfriends (Detail)	182
Water Snakes II	121	Baby	185
The Three Ages of Women	122	Adam and Eve	186
Portrait of Margaret Stonborough-Wittgenstein	125	Dancer	189
The Stoclet Friez (Detail)	126	Bride	190

FABLE

1883
Oil on canvas, 85 x 117 cm
Historisches Museum, Vienna

Fable was painted in 1883, the year that Klimt and his brother Ernst graduated from the Kunstgewerbeschule (School of Arts and Sciences) in Vienna. It resulted from a commission to produce designs for a three volume book entitled Allegories and Emblems, which was intended to update the traditional allegorical language used by artists in order to encompass aspects of modern life, such as commerce and technology. Amongst the other artists who contributed to this prestigious publication were two who were later to be seen as principal rivals to Klimt in the German speaking world – Max Klinger and Franz von Stuck. Though an accomplished piece of work for a twenty one year old, and attractive in its own way, Fable shows no hint of the distinctive style for which Klimt was to become famous more than a decade later. At this stage in his career Klimt was completely under the spell of the so-called "Painter Prince", Hans Mackart, then at the height of his fame and to be forever associated with the pompous overblown historicism of the newly constructed public buildings on the Vienna Ringstrasse. As a student, Klimt had been so in awe of Makart that he and his brother Ernst and their fellow student Franz Matsch bribed Makart's servant to let them into the artist's studio to inspect his vast works while the Master took his siesta.

THE IDYLL

1884
Oil on canvas, 50 x 74 cm
Historisches Museum, Vienna

The Idyll was also painted to illustrate *Allegories* and *Emblems*. Right from the beginning Klimt was a magpie borrower from other artists, and *The Idyll* shows his careful study of the masters of the Italian Renaissance and the Baroque. The muscular male nudes (a rarity in the work of an artist so completely fixated on the female body) derive ultimately from the "Ignudi" in Michelangolo's Sistine Ceiling but also make nodding reference to the trompe l'œil painted male nude sculptures in Annibale Carracci's Farnese Gallery, that seem to project out of the painted surface into real space. For all Klimt's historical references, the physical type of the blonde, female nude in the roundel and the leafy background, reminiscent of a William Morris wallpaper, indicate unmistakably that this is a work of the late nineteenth century. The muted colours of both *Fable* and *The Idyll* reflect not only the musty historicism of contemporary taste but also the fact that these designs were meant for printed reproduction.

THE THEATRE OF TAORMINA

1886-1888
Oil on canvas, 750 x 400 cm
Burgtheater, Vienna

In the 1880s Gustav Klimt, together with his brother Ernst and their friend and former fellow student Franz Matsch, established a reputation for producing large scale decorative schemes for theatres in cities that looked to Vienna for inspiration such as Karlsbad, Bucharest and Fiume. More prestigious still was the commission in 1886 to decorate the ceilings in the two monumental staircases that led to the boxes in the newly constructed Burgtheater on Vienna's Ringstrasse. This magnificent building realised by the veteran theatre architect Gottfried Semper in collaboration with Karl von Hasenauer, was one of a string of buildings that collectively formed an astonishing architectural fancy dress ball around the Ringstrasse in what was, after Haussmann's rebuilding of Paris, the most ambitious scheme of urban renewal in the nineteenth century. With his paintings illustrating the history of theatre from ancient times onwards, Klimt established himself as the legitimate successor to Hans Makart as Vienna's most admired decorator of public spaces. At the same time, though he distanced himself from Makart's old masterful methods by adopting a bright, slick technique closer to that of Parisian academic artists such as Gerome and Bouguereau, and to the brightly coloured and meticulous archaeological reconstructions of the Victorian painter, Sir Lawrence Alma-Tadema. The completion of the Burgtheater scheme was greeted with general praise and marked the highpoint of Klimt's success as a historical painter in conservative art circles. For this work he received the prestigious award of the Gold Cross of Merit.

FEMALE NUDE LYING DOWN

1887-1888
Study for the *Altar of Dionysos*
Black pencil with white highlights, 28.8 x 42.4 cm
Graphische Sammlung Albertina, Vienna

This drawing shows Klimt's thorough grounding in the skills of academic sketching. The model lies in a stationary reclining pose that could be held for hours if necessary, allowing the artist or student to ensure anatomical accuracy and a high degree of finish. It is very different from the momentary and spontaneous poses that Klimt preferred in later years for his rapid life sketches. Years of training, drawing first from plaster casts and later from live models, ensured that nineteenth century artists had highly developed skills, but tended to iron out individuality. This drawing, pleasing and competent though it is, could have been made by almost any academically trained artist, anywhere in Europe. Despite his enormous natural talent, Klimt was surprisingly slow in throwing off his constraining academic background and developing a personal style. It was not until the late 1890s when he was already in his late 30s, that Klimt's distinctive artistic personality began to emerge.

AUDITORIUM OF THE OLD BURGTHEATER

1888
Gouache on paper, 82 x 92 cm
Historisches Museum, Vienna

Klimt's 1888 gouache of the auditorium in the Old Burgtheater provides a valuable document, not only of the Viennese theatre-going public of his day but also of the historic theatre in which Mozart's Marriage of Figaro had first been performed in 1786. Unfortunately, the theatre was later demolished to make way for the pompous new wing of the Hofburg palace. Despite the quasi-photographic realism of the individual figures the overall effect of this picture is curiously stilted and artificial as if it were an elaborate collage, with the figures not interacting with one another or even inhabiting the same space. Far removed from the exciting and innovative styles that Klimt would develop a decade later, or indeed that Van Gogh and Gauguin were developing in France in that very year, this meticulous and skilful gouache found favour with the arbiters of official taste in Vienna. In 1890 it won the artist the Emperor's Prize of 4,000 guilders.

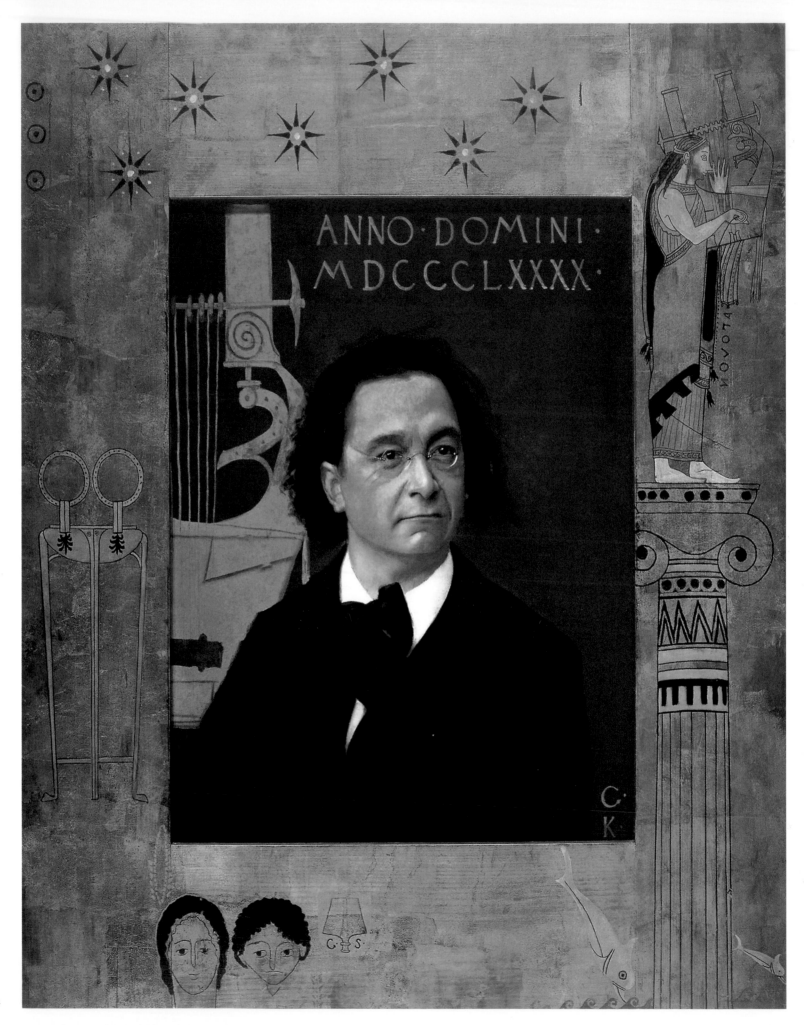

PORTRAIT OF JOSEPH PEMBAUR

1890
Oil on canvas, 69 x 55 cm
Tiroler Landesmuseum Ferdinandeum, Innsbruck

Portraits of men are extremely rare in Klimt's works. During his later years Klimt would only accept commissions to paint the portraits of beautiful women. The decidedly unattractive Joseph Pembauer would seem to have been an unlikely subject for Klimt. The convivial pianist, teacher and composer was honoured by the creation of the "Pembauer Society" whose members gathered on a Thursday at the Löwenbräu tavern in Vienna. It was for this Pembauer Society that Klimt painted this small portrait in 1890. Like several of his portraits of around this time, it gives the impression of having been painted from a photograph rather than from life. As in the spandrel decorations for the staircase of the Kunsthistorische Museum which he was painting at the same time, Klimt places the strongly three-dimensional figure against a flatly decorative background. Perhaps the most interesting feature of the picture is its decorative frame. We see the results of the study Klimt made of ancient Greek vases while researching for his murals for the Kunsthistorischesmseum, in his use of the Delphic tripod that Klimt lifted from a fifth century BCE Attic red figure vase. He would re-use this motif later in his design for a cover of Ver Sacrum, the magazine of the Vienna Secession.

ANCIENT GREEK ART I

1890-1891
Oil on plaster, 230 x 230 cm
Kunsthistorisches Museum, Vienna

Klimt's position as the successor to Makart was yet more clearly established when he inherited the commission to complete the decorations of the staircase of the Kunsthistorische Museum which had been left unfinished when Makart died in 1884. Gustav, Ernst Klimt and Franz Matsch provided forty paintings illustrating the development of art from ancient Egypt, until the Renaissance, in order to decorate the spandrels and the awkward narrow, vertical spaces between the columns. In the eleven panels painted by Gustav Klimt himself between 1890 and 1891, we have the first intimations of his impending break with academic orthodoxy and of the direction he would move in by the end of the decade. The very awkwardness of the panel shapes which did not lend itself to an effective representation of spatial recession may have encouraged Klimt to paint in a flatter and more compressed and stylised manner. For the first time we see that juxtaposition of almost photographically rendered elements (notably the faces) with flat, decorative backgrounds. For the first time, too, Klimt moved on from the passive and rather bovine feminine ideal of academic art, to a female type with some of the "femme fatale" allure that characterises his later depictions of woman.

THE LOVE

1895
Oil on canvas, 60 x 44 cm
Kunsthistorisches Museum, Vienna

The theme of an embracing couple would be dealt with more memorably by Klimt on several later occasions, most notably in his design for the mosaic frieze in the Stoclet Palace, in the *Beethoven Frieze* and above all in what became his most popular work *The Kiss* of 1907-1909 In 1895, when Klimt painted this delicate picture, it was a mere two years before the founding of the Vienna Secession and Klimt's own sudden transformation from a conservative academic painter into the standard bearer of the Viennese avant-garde. But Klimt's treatment of the embracing figures is still essentially academic and surprisingly unadventurous. In the sinister floating figures at the top of the canvas we have an interesting foretaste of the Vienna University ceilings as well as of the *Beethoven Frieze*. The frame, with its extensive use of flat gilding, the asymmetrical and cropped placing of the roses, shows clearly that Klimt was already intrigued by the principles of Japanese design, though the roses themselves have cabbage-like Western three-dimensionality.

MUSIC I

1895
Oil, gold and bronze on canvas, 27.5 x 35.5 cm
Neue Pinakothek, Munich

Music was the most widely loved of the arts in Vienna at the turn of the century. Vienna was still regarded as the musical capital of the world. It was the city of Mozart, Beethoven and Schubert and more recently of Brahms, the Strauss family, Bruckner and Mahler. In 1897 Gustav Mahler took over the direction of the Imperial Opera and brought something new to the musical life of Vienna in much the same way that the founding of the Secession did in the same year. Mahler's provocative declaration, "Tradition is sloppiness" paralleled the more elegantly phrased motto, "To every age its art, to art its freedom" that adorned the façade of the new Secession building. *Music I* of 1895 is stylistically far in advance of *Love* painted in the same year. Indeed *Music I* was one of Klimt's first exercises in the manner shortly to be dubbed the "Secession style". A second version of three years later was paired with Schubert at the piano to decorate the music room of the Palais Dumba.

FINAL DRAWING FOR THE
ALLEGORY OF TRAGEDY

1897
Black chalk, wash, gold and white highlights, 42 x 31 cm
Kunsthistorisches Museum, Vienna

Fourteen years after the publisher Martin Gerlach gave him his first major opportunity by commissioning designs for his *Allegories* and *Emblems* pieces, he returned to Klimt for a second set of designs that were produced between 1895 and 1897. A comparison between *Fable* of 1883 and *Tragedy* of 1897, this work highlights the remarkable transformation that had taken place in Klimt's work. The two designs could be by quite different artists. The sinister beauty of the tragic muse Melpomene, shows Klimt's interest in the Belgian Symbolist Fernand Khnopff, then at the height of his fame. The gilded collar that appears to sever Melpomene's head from her body and which would become such a feature of Klimt's depiction of women over the next few years, was also originally derived from Khnopff.

FISH BLOOD

1898
Illustration for the magazine *Ver Sacrum*
Ink on paper

This black and white drawing was first published in 1898 in the *Ver Sacrum*. It is one of Klimt's first pictures in which he focuses on the depiction of the female body as well as the characteristics of moving water. These motifs reappear in several later, very similar artworks such as the painting *Moving Water* (1898) which, however, is dominated by dark and brooding shades of green instead of the sober black and white of *The Blood of Fish* . Klimt would take up the theme of female bodies and moving water again, much later, in *Water Serpents I* (1904-1907). *Fish Blood* shows four nude female figures who are drifting light-heartedly, nearly motionless on a fast-flowing stream, that cuts diagonally through the composition of the drawing. In contrast to the other figures, the fourth woman lacks the grace of the other three and looks like she is rather swept along by the stream, like human flotsam, while clinging to the oversized head of a fish. This fish head seems to indicate that the whole scene is not happening on the surface of a stream but rather deep underwater. A similar fish head also appears in the later painting *Goldfish* (1901-1902) where it similarly observes floating female figures with its empty eyes. This fish, which is not completely visible in the picture, can be interpreted as a masculine symbol. It takes on the negatively connotated role of the observer, the voyeur who silently watches the activities of the women. The women's long hair follows the lines of the stream, not unlike algae. All of the female figures are turned towards the viewer so that their hairless pubic regions are visible. Their genitalia are only indicated by a slight "V" line that was commonly used at that time. The eroticism of the female figures in this painting has been freed from all social conventions and boundaries dictated by the predominant moral dogma of that time; a new development in Klimt's works. In this painting the female bodies merge with the surrounding nature, lazily following the current and offering no resistance.

COMPOSITIONAL PROJECT FOR MEDICINE

1897-1898
Oil on canvas, 72 x 55 cm
Private collection, Vienna

Apart from photographs and preparatory drawings this is all that remains as evidence of the appearance of the first of the three great ceiling paintings for the University of Vienna that were amongst Klimt's greatest achievements. In 1891 following the much acclaimed success of the decorative schemes for the Burgtheater and the Kunsthistorischesmuseum, Klimt and Franz Matsch were commissioned to paint a series of monumental panels to decorate the great hall of the University of Vienna. Matsch was to paint the central panel representing "The Victory of Light over Darkness" and a panel representing Theology (presumably this subject was thought unsuitable for the notoriously hedonistic Klimt). Klimt undertook the painting of the three remaining panels to symbolise the university faculties of philosophy, medicine and jurisprudence. When the first of the panels, *Philosophy*, was exhibited in 1900, the mature Klimt was revealed to the world on a monumental scale for the first time. Though the panel was warmly praised and won a gold medal when it was exhibited at the 1900 Paris world fair, conservative Vienna proved less understanding of the new direction in which Klimt was travelling. The second panel, *Medicine*, caused outrage when it was exhibited in 1901, with its disturbing eroticism and its blatant depiction of female pubic hair (something quite unprecedented in Western art in a public work of this nature).

In response to the continuing controversy, Klimt eventually paid back his advance from the university and retained ownership of the three paintings. Tragically, in one of the great artistic losses of the Second World War, the panels were destroyed when Immendorf Castle, where they were being stored for safety, was deliberately burned by the retreating SS troops.

PALLAS ATHENA

1898
Oil on canvas, 75 x 75 cm
Historisches Museum, Vienna

Around the turn of the century, many leading cultural figures in German speaking countries showed renewed and intense interest in ancient Greek culture and mythology, from Freud and Hofmannsthal through to the composer Richard Strauss and the painters Franz von Stuck and Gustav Klimt. They were looking for profound and universal meanings in an ancient culture in which the entire Western tradition had its origins. One of the first examples of Klimt's fully developed "Secession" style, *Pallas Athena* was shown at the second exhibition of the Vienna Secession in 1898. It brings Klimt close to his Bavarian contemporary Franz von Stuck who was the dominant figure of the Munich Secession that preceded that of Vienna by four years. Stuck also depicted Athena amongst many other Greek subjects. With many stylistic elements in common as well as careers that paralleled one another in their respective cities, Klimt and Stuck were inevitably compared. Hofmannsthal was convinced that Stuck's was the more profound and genuine talent and that Klimt was merely meretricious and modish. He would no doubt have been surprised to see how time has reversed this judgement.

The sculptured frame which is integral to the picture was designed by Klimt and made by his brother Georg.

PORTRAIT OF SONJA KNIPS

1898
Oil on canvas, 141 x 141 cm
Österreichische Galerie Belvedere, Vienna

The *Portrait of Sonja Knips* was shown at the second exhibition of the Vienna Secession in 1898 and was an early example of Klimt's remarkable ability to synthesise disparate stylistic elements into something utterly individual and distinctive. The dominant influences here are from Japanese woodblock prints and from Whistler (an artist who had already shown how to incorporate Japanese elements into Western portraits). The Japanese influence is apparent in the startling asymmetry of the composition, the use of empty spaces as positive compositional elements (notably in the spaces between the sitter's arms and torso as well as the large empty space on the left of the picture) and the strange intrusion of flowers into the picture space from the left and the right. Klimt could have seen a similar use of flowers in Whistler's *Portrait of Cecily Alexander*. Whistler's influence also shows itself in the delicately muddy, soft-focus technique and in the muted and exquisite colour harmony. The sweet femininity of the sitter is counteracted by features that introduce elements of tension into the picture, such as the suggestion of a grotesque mask in the background, the tense claw-like pose of her left hand on the arm of the chair and the mysterious little red book she holds so tentatively in her right hand.

EXHIBITION WALLPAPER FOR SECESSION I

1898 (before censure)
Lithograph, 63.5 x 46.9 cm
Museum of Modern Art, New York

James McNeill Whistler ended his famous "Ten o'clock lecture" with the ringing declaration that the story of beauty is complete "written in the marbles of the Parthenon and embroidered on the fan of Hokusai". The challenge of this strange juxtaposition of ancient Greece and Japan is taken up in this poster which combines profile figures inspired by Greek vase painting with an extreme asymmetry and a use of empty space derived from Japanese woodblock prints. The subject of the slaying of the Minotaur by Theseus may be read as intended to represent the struggle of the Vienna Secession against the forces of philistinism and conservatism. Viennese officialdom struck back by forcing Klimt to censor the conspicuously displayed genitalia of Theseus. In a second version of the poster, Klimt complied with the censorship, but not by falling back on the clichéd device of the fig leaf. Instead, he cheekily and ingeniously introduced a further Japanese design element with an asymmetrically placed tree trunk that conveniently covered the offending parts.

NUDA VERITAS

1899
Oil on canvas, 252 x 56 cm
Theatersammlung der Nationalbibliothek, Vienna

I n *Nuda Veritas*, which was exhibited at the fourth exhibition of the Vienna Secession in March 1899, we see brought together all the elements that we associate with the Secession style. Klimt finally achieved a satisfactory synthesis of naturalistic and abstract, decorative elements.

The text on the gilded ground and the surrounding frame are integral to the composition. The frontally posed nude with her halo of fiery hair, her somewhat sinister allure and her explicitly depicted pubic hair conform to what would be from now on Klimt's feminine ideal.

The image of naked truth and the provocative quote from Schiller, "If by your actions and your art you cannot please everyone – please a few. To please everyone is bad", refers not only to Klimt's rejection of the hypocrisy of conservative Vienna, but also (according to Klimt's friend Bertha Zuckerkandl), expresses his response to the contemporary struggle for truth in France by the supporters of the unjustly accused Captain Dreyfus. As Klimt's major patrons and supporters were almost exclusively Jewish, it is hardly surprising that Klimt should have sympathised with the Dreyfusards. It was the Dreyfus Affair that shocked the Viennese journalist Theodor Herzl into abandoning his hopes for the assimilation of Jews into European society and inspired his call for the founding of a Jewish state.

NUDA VERITAS (DETAIL)

1899
Oil on canvas, 252 x 56 cm
Theatersammlung der Nationalbibliothek, Vienna

The life-sized but narrow and elongated painting *Nuda Veritas* is headlined by a quote from Friedrich Schiller (1759-1805), taken from a votive tablet: "If you cannot please everyone through your deeds and your art, only please a select few; Trying to please everyone, is a dire thing to do".

The text that frames the depicted scene is an integral part of the artwork. The central piece is the frontally shown nude figure which, with her flower-adorned hair and the explicitly shown pubic hair, seems to radiate with eerie attractiveness. She stands on a pedestal; out of the underground a snake wreathes itself around the feet of the woman into the mid-blue haze that seem to hover above the pedestal. Two flowers are growing right beside the woman and the blue changes into a light blue and merges with the darkening background. At her shoulders golden ornamental lines sprout out of the borders and coil themselves into forms that almost seem to resemble a shepherd's staff.

Ludwing Hevesi (1842-1910), one of the most famous Austrian journalists, art critics and writers of that decade, made the following comment on *Nuda Veritas:*

In general, Klimt's "Nuda Veritas" painting is a playful take on Symbolist tendencies. Vague sensations just flow freely instead of making the effort to form itself into a coherent thought. This is mirrored by the playful way the brush touches the form; it is caressing the vague instead of forming a clear outline. This whole piece of imagination is, as a chemist might say, just a by-product, a waste product of the big *Hygieia* painting meant for the festival room of the Vienna University. The whirl of design ideas, which is raging through the mind of the artist in the process of creation, produces from time to time a more concrete form, which, however, only takes on a slight glint of meaning. That is how the "Veritas" came to be...

SCHUBERT AT PIANO

1899
Oil on canvas, 150 x 200 cm
Burnt in 1945 at Immendorf Castle

Schubert at the Piano was commissioned to decorate the music room in the Palais Dumba. The elongated, horizontal format of the picture indicates that, like its pendent *Music II*, it was intended to be placed above a door.

Though the high waistlines of the young women's dresses follow the fashion of the early nineteenth century Biedermeier period in which Schubert lived, their facial types and hair styles are very much of Klimt's own time.

The patterned broken brushwork Klimt has used in this picture indicates his familiarity with the Neo-Impressionist techniques of Seurat and his followers but is used somewhat differently to create a flatter more decorative effect. This charming picture which was amongst the most popular and successful of Klimt's works during his lifetime, was, like the university ceilings, lost in the conflagration at Immendorf Castle in 1945.

TWO LOVERS

1901-1902
Study for the *Beethoven Frieze*
Black pencil, 45 x 30.8 cm
Vienna

This drawing is a study for the section of the *Beethoven Frieze* entitled somewhat euphemistically *The Yearning for Happiness finds Fulfillment in Happiness*. Ostensibly this section of the Frieze connects with Schiller's *Ode to Joy* sung by soloists and full chorus in the last movement of Beethoven's *Ninth Symphony*. The floating virgins lined up on either side of the embracing couple in the frieze might be seen as representing Beethoven's chorus.

As in *The Kiss* painted several years later, the abstract, decorative surroundings of the couple suggest fairly explicitly the form of an erect phallus within the surrounding vagina. In the painting itself, the veil surrounding the feet of the couple adds to the piquancy by emphasising their nakedness and the urgency of their embrace. The male nude is a rare exception in Klimt's art. The rippling musculature of his back is somewhat reminiscent of the back of the male figure in Rodin's sculpture *The Kiss*.

ISLAND ON THE ATTERSEE

c.1901
Oil on canvas, 100 x 100 cm
Private collection

For over twenty years Klimt enjoyed spending the summer months with his lover Emilie Flöge and her family by the Attersee. A great lover of boating, Klimt, like Monet before him, enjoyed the luxury of painting nature from the undisturbed privacy of a boat, though Klimt was never as concerned as Monet or Sisley with the direct transposition of nature onto the surface of the canvas. The composition of this picture suggests that it may have been painted on, rather than beside, the Attersee. The luminous palette of colours and the use of broken brushwork to render the shimmering surface of the water, show Klimt's knowledge of Monet's work even before it was shown at the Secession in 1903. The oriental compositional device of the extremely high horizon line, used to flatten space, was also used by Monet in the later stages of his career.

GOLDFISH

1902
Oil on canvas, 181 x 66.5 cm
Kunstmuseum Solothurn, Solothurn

G*oldfish* presents female sexuality as something at once fascinating and menacing. The smiles of the floating women are both enticing and chilling. Their coquettishness is reminiscent of the Rhinemaidens in the opening scene of Wagner's *Das Rheingold*. They are all endowed with an abundance of flowing hair – the ultimate weapon of seduction. At a time when respectable women kept their hair up and under careful control in public situations, the sight of such free-flowing hair held connotations of the loss of inhibitions and unbridled sexuality. In the late nineteenth century and up to the First World War artists such as Dante Gabriel Rossetti, Burne-Jones, Beardsley, Waterhouse, Degas, Munch, Mucha, Toorop and Klimt himself, indulged in fetishist fantasies of women's hair.

Just as hair could be used to envelop, entrap and even suffocate or strangle, water too had connotations of dangerous sexuality and drowning and was often associated with femme fatales and sirens. The elongated vertical format of this painting, foreign to the Western tradition, derives ultimately from Chinese scroll painting via Japanese woodblock prints.

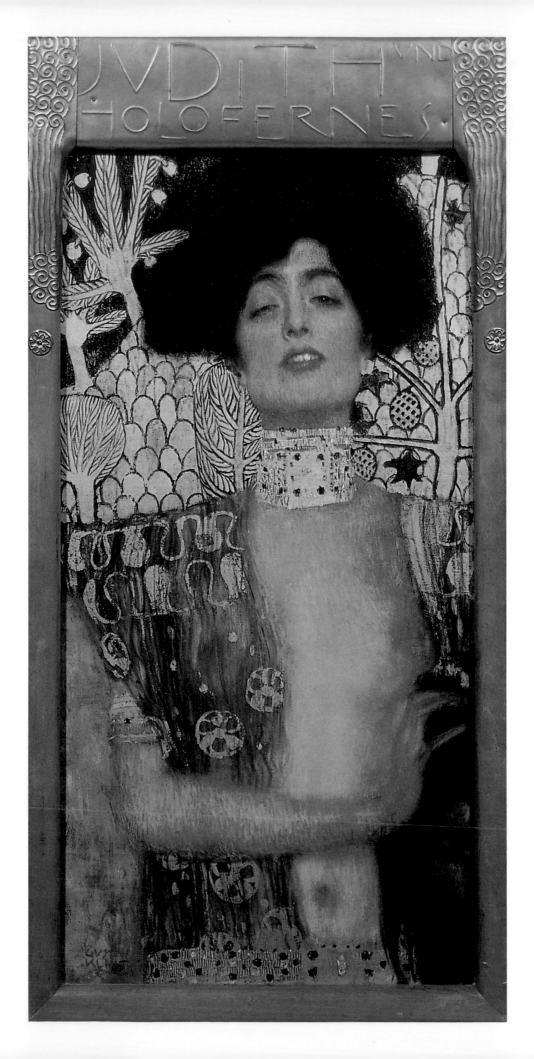

JUDITH I

1901
Oil on canvas, 84 x 42 cm
Österreichische Galerie Belvedere, Vienna

The biblical heroine Judith saved the Jewish people by seducing and slaying the Philistine general Holofernes. Renaissance artists such as Donatello used her as an archetype of patriotism and female courage. In the seventeenth century, Baroque artists such as Caravaggio, Johannes Liss and Artemesis Gentileschi began to explore the psychosexual possibilities of the subject, but it was not until the late nineteenth century that Judith was elevated, alongside Salome, to the status of a fully-fledged femme fatale. Amongst the other artists of this period who depicted Judith in the role of Femme Fatale were Franz von Stuck, and Gustave Mossa. Klimt's *Judith I* of 1901 is perhaps the most powerful and disturbing of all his depictions of menacing female sexuality. With her raised head, crowned by an abundance of hair, her strong chin, half-closed eyes and parted lips creating an expression of ecstasy, Klimt's Judith descends (perhaps via the Belgian symbolist Fernand Khnopff) from Dante Gabriel Rossetti's influential *Beata Beatrix*. She is also related to Munch's *Madonna* and the girl in Mucha's *Job* poster, though the ecstasy of Mucha's young lady is prompted by nothing more sinister than a drag on a cigarette. The jewelled collar that appears to sever Judith's own head is also a feature of many of Klimt's portraits of these years.

PORTRAIT OF GERTHA FELSOVANYI

1902
Oil on canvas, 150 x 45.5 cm
Private collection

In this 1902 portrait Klimt returns to the almost life-sized rectangular format that he had previously used on *Nuda Veritas* in 1899. In the same year Klimt painted Gertha Felsovanyi he also made the *Portrait of Serena Lederer*, the wife an industrial magnate from Austria, making these two artworks the first portraits he painted in years. The lack of portraits in the years from 1898 to 1902 can be easily explained: Klimt concentrated all his efforts on the assignment for the *Beethoven Frieze*, which had to be finished in time for the 14th Exhibition of the Vienna Secession. There is hardly any information on the person of Gertha Felsovanyi. It is unclear who she was, where she came from and where her life went after this portrait. It is almost as if Klimt had a premonition that this information would not last for the ages: the portrait of Gertha Felsovanyi is characterized by its paleness, fragility and haziness of its central figure. Was it her own wish to be portrayed in that manner or was it an affliction that gave her this frail appearance? She seems to almost want to step out of the painting and yet remains distant and inapproachable. Gertha Felsovanyi stands upright but the outline of her figure is diffused and almost dissolves in the "spaceless" background. What might be reason for the lack of detail in the background that would let the beholder know where the figure is standing? It is also striking that her feet remain invisible while her full, brown hair touches the upper boundary of the painting. She looks directly at the beholder with big, sad eyes. Lips and cheeks seem flushed in an almost unnatural shade of red. Gertha's body is veiled from top to bottom, her figure indistinct. There are no arms or legs visible; only her folded hands that appear out of the depths of her patterned green dress. Klimt, who is usually rather clear and even explicit in his depiction of women, remains unusually vague in his depiction of Gertha Felsovanyi.

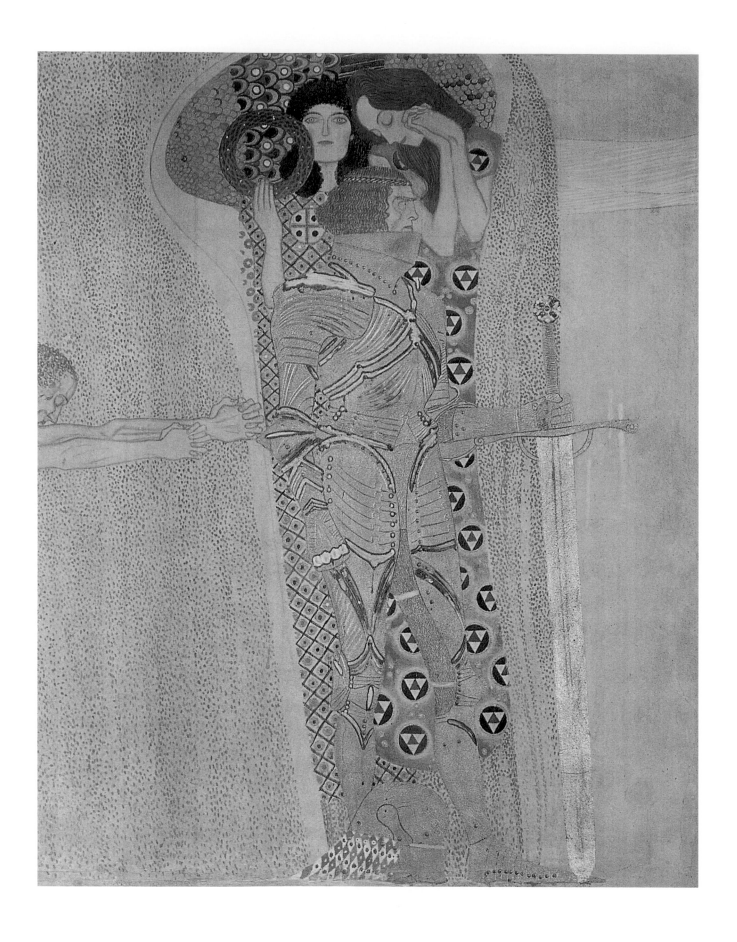

THE BEETHOVEN FRIEZE: AMBITION, COMPASSION AND THE KNIGHT IN SHINING ARMOR (DETAIL)

1902
Casein on plaster, height: 220 cm
Secession, Vienna

By default, following the tragic destruction of the Vienna University ceilings, the *Beethoven Frieze* has become Klimt's most important surviving work. Indeed the unexpected and near miraculous survival of this vast and fragile work painted on plaster that was never meant to be permanent, makes up to some extent for the losses of the Second World War.

The *Beethoven Frieze* was intended as a backdrop for Klinger's ten-foot-high polychrome sculpture of Beethoven that was shown at the fourteenth exhibition of the Vienna Secession in 1902. A near contemporary of Klimt and Stuck, Max Klinger is chiefly admired today as a quirkily original printmaker. His paintings paralleled those of Klimt in attempting to combine elements of disparate styles, but are far less successful in synthesising the mythological subject matter and heavy symbolism of Bocklin with the plein-air palette of the Impressionists.

The *Beethoven* statue, once regarded as one of the peaks of Western art, now seems more of a monument to bad taste and megalomania than to Beethoven. Its overblown monumentalism is disturbingly prescient of the art of the Third Reich.

Klimt's Frieze pays little deference either to Klinger or indeed to Beethoven. Instead Klimt explores his standard theme of human and above all female sexuality.

PORTRAIT OF EMILIE FLÖGE

1902
Oil on canvas, 181 x 84 cm
Historisches Museum, Vienna

Klimt never married and by all accounts does not seem to have been bound by conventional concepts of sexual fidelity, but nevertheless maintained a long-term relationship with Emilie Flöge that lasted until his death. Emilie Flöge and her sisters (one of whom was married to Klimt's brother Ernst) ran a fashion house in Vienna called the Casa Piccolo. As a believer in the Arts and Crafts doctrine of the unity of fine and decorative arts inherited from William Morris and practised by other contemporary artist designers such as Henri van de Velde and Charles Rennie Mackintosh, Klimt was happy to work in Emilie Flöge's fashion business and did not regard the designing of dresses, textiles and even labels as being beneath him. Emilie Flöge's loose but streamlined gown is very different from the tightly corseted look of Sonja Knips' dress painted four years earlier and still visible in well-known photographs of fashionable ladies visiting the Vienna Kunstschau in 1908. Emilie's sumptuous gown lies somewhere between the aesthetic garb of the Pre-Raphaelite women and the revolutionary corset-less designs produced by the Parisian couturier Paul Poiret after 1908. The use of silvered geometric elements marks the beginning of Klimt's Byzantine or "golden" style that would reach a climax five years later with his first portrait of Adele Bloch-Bauer.

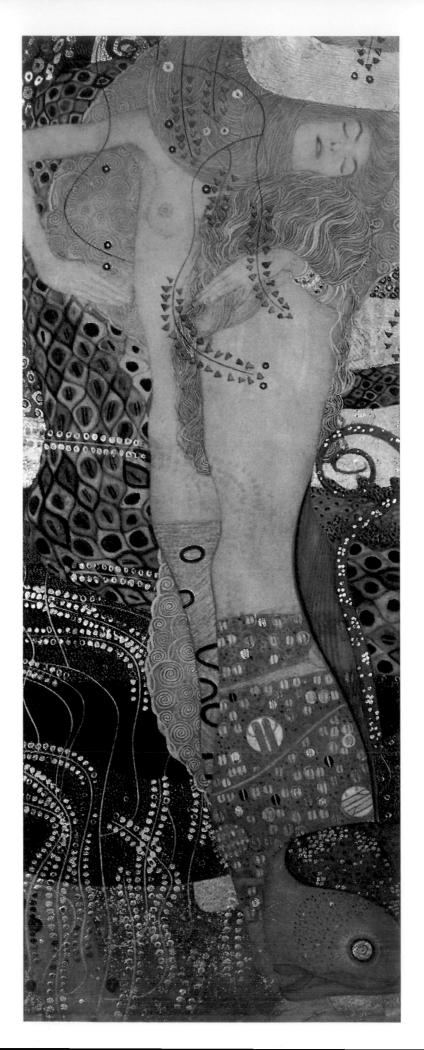

WATER SNAKES I

1904-1907
Mixed technique, watercolour and gold on parchment, 50 x 20 cm
Österreichische Galerie Belvedere, Vienna

Klimt's frank exploration of female sexuality makes him seem very modern. But there are many ways in which his art is firmly rooted in the nineteenth century. It is enough to remember that in 1907, the year Klimt completed this exquisite and precious work on parchment that Picasso was working on that cornerstone of Modernism, *Les Demoiselles d'Avignon (the Young Ladies of Avignon)*, to realise that the visual language that Klimt used to the end of his life, was essentially that of the fin de siècle. The theme of the mermaid or siren was a popular one in nineteenth century art, literature and opera. Klimt would have been very familiar with Arnold Bocklin's paintings of frolicking mermaids that were immensely famous in the German speaking world, though Böcklin's hausfrau-like sirens are very different from Klimt's svelte and alluring creatures.

The extreme and anatomically impossible torsion of the upper mermaid's neck is a feature found in several of Klimt's paintings such as *The Kiss*, *The Virgin* and the unfinished *The Bride* and seems to denote ecstasy.

WATER SNAKES II

1904-1907
Oil on canvas, 80 x 145 cm
Private collection

For many viewers in the early 1900s the most shocking feature of this picture, as well as of *Hope I* would have been Klimt's unabashed depiction of the golden haze of pubic hair. Female pubic hair was one of the great unmentionable and unrepresentable subjects of the nineteenth century and indeed had hardly ever been depicted in Western art before Klimt, outside of pornography. It was a topic of intense interest to nineteenth century male libertines as we know from the Paris guide books for sexual tourists that describe the pubic hair of available women in the most specific anatomical detail. As early as the 1860s Courbet had painted a close up view of the unwaxed female pudenda that he entitled *L'Origine du Monde (The Origin of the World)* but this was made for the private delectation of a Turkish collector of erotica rather then for pubic exhibition.

After a lifetime of studying Western art, the British historian and critic John Ruskin was so disconcerted to discover on his wedding night that women also have pubic hair that he was unable to consummate the marriage. After 1900, thanks to Klimt, this was not a problem likely to afflict Viennese art lovers.

THE THREE AGES OF WOMEN

1905
Oil on canvas, 178 x 198 cm
Galleria Nazionale d'Arte Moderna, Rome

The ageing process and in particular that of women was a traditional subject and had been depicted by Renaissance artists such as Hans Baldung Grien and Giorgione. The human life cycle was a common preoccupation of artists of the Symbolist era. Klimt would have been familiar with Arnold Böcklin. 1888 painting *Vita somnuium breve* that deals with the stages of life from babyhood to death and also with Munch's 1894 *The Three Stages of Woman* that deals somewhat misogynistically with the three aspects of woman as virgin, whore and death rather than with the ageing process as such. Klimt's tender and painfully honest treatment of the aged woman is perhaps the most remarkable feature of this picture. He may have been inspired by Rodin's moving depiction of the frailty of age in his small bronze entitled, *She Who Was Once the Helmet-Maker's Beautiful Wife.* Fourteen of Rodin's sculptures were included in the tenth exhibition of the Vienna Secession in 1901. Though Klimt would later develop a looser and more painterly technique, his careful delineation of the complex, knotty anatomy of the old woman and the hatched shading of her concave buttock, show that he was always essentially a draughtsman who painted, rather than a lover of belle peinture for its own sake.

PORTRAIT OF MARGARET STONBOROUGH-WITTGENSTEIN

1905
Oil on canvas, 179.8 x 90.5 cm
Neue Pinakothek, Munich

Margaret Stonborough-Wittgenstein belonged to those wealthy and highly cultured assimilated Jewish families who provided Klimt with most of his patrons and who indeed were the very backbone of Viennese culture during its brief and dazzling "golden age" between 1890 and the First World War.

This portrait met the fate of so many commissioned society portraits in failing to please the sitter. Two years after this portrait was painted, the king of society portraitists, John Singer Sargent gave up taking commissions of women, commenting bitterly that a portrait is just a picture of someone in which the mouth is "not quite right". Klimt was required to make alterations before he could collect his handsome fee of 5,000 guilders. Although this portrait is relatively restrained compared to many of Klimt's other paintings of the period, the highly-minded and intellectual Stonborough-Wittgenstein, may have been averse to Klimt's highly ornamented style. Later she would commission her famous philosopher brother Ludwig Wittgenstein to design for her a villa in a severe, functionalist style that consciously reacted to the Byzantine excesses of the Vienna Secession.

THE STOCLET FRIEZE
(DETAIL)

1905-1912
Mixed technique, oil on canvas, 197 x 91 cm
Österreichisches Museum für Angewandte Kunst, Vienna

t is ironic that the most lavish and complete example of the Vienna Secession style survives not in Vienna itself but in a city associated with a very different kind of Art Nouveau. This is the so called Palais Stoclet on the outskirts of Brussels, commissioned by the Belgian financier Adolphe Stoclet who had lived in Vienna and chose the Viennese architect Josef Hoffmann rather than Victor Horta, the local master of the curvilinear Belgian Art Nouveau style. Every element within the house, down to the cutlery that graced the dining table, was created by Viennese artists and designers associated with the Secession and the Wiener Werkstätte. For the dining room, Klimt designed a magnificent mosaic, executed by Leopold Forstner in precious metals, semi-precious stones, enamel and coral against a background of white marble.

The richly decorative mosaic relates to the Byzantine style of paintings such as *The Kiss* and the first portrait of Adele Bloch-Bauer, painted around the same time. The theme of expectation and fulfilment once again shows Klimt's obsessive interest in human sexuality.

SUNFLOWER GARDEN

c. 1906
Oil on canvas, 110 x 110 cm
Österreichische Galerie Belvedere, Vienna

The all-over density of detail of this painting gives the impression that the painting is a section of sumptuous wallpaper. The cropping of the plants and flowers on all four sides of the canvas implies that we are looking at a tiny fragment of nature that continues infinitely in all directions. In this painting that probably reflects the unkempt profusion of Klimt's own garden, the artist wishes to celebrate the sheer fecundity of nature.

Van Gogh's paintings had been shown at the Secession in 1903 and by this time his paintings of sunflowers were already legendary. Though Klimt undoubtedly knew them, there is no indication from this painting that he paid much attention to them. Klimt's flowers are more purely decorative and less charged with subjective emotion than those of Van Gogh.

This picture was first shown at the 1908 Vienna Kunstschau, the exhibition that revealed the more abrasive talents of a younger generation of Viennese artists who certainly had paid attention to Van Gogh, which included Egon Schiele, Oskar Kokoschka and Richard Gerstl. In the company of these firebrands, Klimt himself was elevated to the status of a living old master.

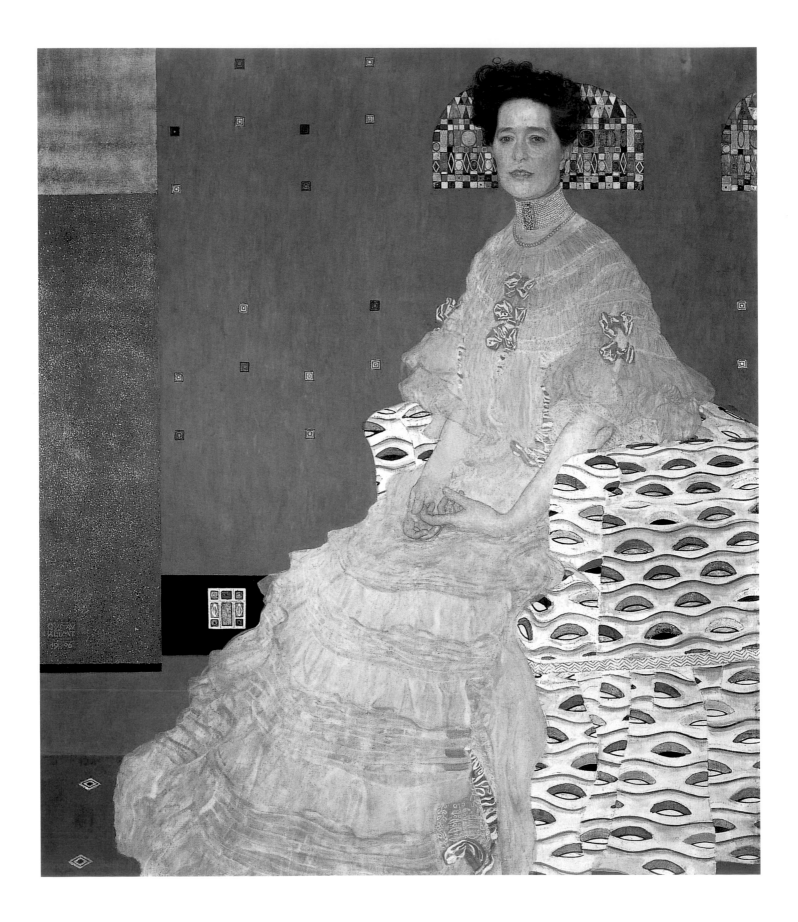

PORTRAIT OF FRITZA RIEDLER

1906
Oil on canvas, 152 x 134 cm
Österreichische Galerie Belvedere, Vienna

In his *Portrait of Fritza Riedler*, Klimt further develops the deliberate tension between the naturalism and three dimensional depiction of the face and the hands and the surrounding flat and geometric decorative elements that seem to imprison the figure.

The elliptical "eye" motif, which may be seen as symbolically representing the female sex organ, would become a constant feature of Klimt's work over the next few years. The spatially ambiguous semi-circular mosaic panel behind Fritza Riedler's head draws attention to her face and also makes witty reference to the elaborate headdresses of the Spanish Habsburg princesses in the famous Velázquez portraits in the Kunsthistorisches Museum in Vienna. This portrait is yet another example of Klimt's creative and brilliant eclecticism. We have an unlikely but highly successful fusion of elements taken from Spanish Baroque painting, Byzantine mosaics, Japanese wood block prints and in some of the geometric decoration, ancient Greek art.

MEDICINE

1900-1907
Oil on canvas, 430 x 300 cm
Burnt in 1945 at Immendorf Castle

The painting has an unusually long history that began in 1848 with the planning for a new building for the University of Vienna. After a long fight, that was spearheaded by the professors of the university, the building was finally inaugurated in 1883 although the interior was not yet finished. The newest addition to the campus was still missing the artistic decoration that was supposed to portray the favoured academic disciplines of the teaching body. After extensive groundwork and a multitude of design suggestions, Franz Matsch and Gustav Klimt received the definitive order to complete the panels. The nature of this commission is easily understood: the University expected a series of formal, dignified artworks in a classical style which were supposed to portray the healing power of medical science, the wisdom of the philosopher and undoubtedly the robed figure of Justice holding scales with blindfolded eyes representing law and jurisprudence. After a few years of hard work however, the university received such a controversial painting that it immediately caused a scandal and sparked wild debates over its appropriateness.

It is hard to say what Klimt wanted to express with this painting. The vision that the painting is conveying is chaotic, almost hellishly bleak. The skulls of old and wrinkled figures and the randomly scattered people rather attest to the decay and suffering of the human body than to its healing. The figure at the bottom with the snake wrapped around her arm is meant to represent the concept of medicine. Her portrayal, however, in her ornamental garment rather evokes the image of priestess that is sacrificing the sick. The other female figure which is positioned beside the pillar of the human bodies and silhouettes is notable for her posture: Her arms are thrown out as if mockingly imitating the crucifixion. This work also represents a complete break with the tradition of depicting round and homely women that were predominant in the academic style of the nineteenth century. Klimt paints his women with long hair and lean, curvy bodies. Their sexual confidence makes them attractive but – in its directness – menacing at the same time.

HYGIEIA
(DETAIL OF MEDICINE)

1900-1907
Oil on canvas, 430 x 300 cm
Burnt in 1945 at Immendorf Castle

The Hippocratic oath beings with the words: "I swear by Apollo, the healer, Asclepius, Hygieia, and Panacea, and I take to witness all the gods, all the goddesses...,"

In the mythology of Ancient Greece, Hygieia was known as the daughter of Asclepius, granddaughter of Apollo and the goddess of health, cleanliness and sanitary facilities. Furthermore she is also the patron goddess of pharmacists, presumably because of the cornucopia that is said to be filled with medicines, crowns and ducats, which is visible on many statues portraying her. Panacea was her sister who was worshipped as the goddess of medicine and magic, two disciplines that sometimes seem quite indistinguishable from each other. In Klimt's works she can be seen on the panel *Medicine* (1901) where she is one of the clearly recognizable figures at the bottom of a pillar of human bodies. She is carrying her head held high, her thick auburn hair is adorned with stylized flowers, and her eyes are half-closed. Yet she seems to be looking down on the viewer. Her head is turned towards the light. She is wearing a red garment that is patterned with golden ornaments. A snake is coiling itself around her right forearm and lowering its head into a bowl that Hygieia is carrying in her left hand. The image of the snake and the bowl, usually referred to as "Bowl of Hygieia", is one of the many symbols associated with the practice of pharmacy.

PORTRAIT OF ADELE BLOCH-BAUER I

1907
Oil, gold and silver leaf on canvas, 140 x 140 cm
Neue Galerie, New York

In 1903 on a trip to Ravenna, Klimt was greatly impressed by the famous early Christian mosaics in the churches of the city. The results of that interest were seen in his so-called Byzantine or Golden style that he developed over the next few years, using collage-like patterns of gold and silver ornament applied to the surface of the canvas. A tendency to flatness and abstraction had been common in much of Western avant-garde painting in the late nineteenth century from Manet and Rossetti onwards. What is unusual about Klimt's style is the combination of naturalistic elements with large areas of abstract geometrical ornament. Once again, much of this is symbolically and erotically charged and we find the vaginal "eye" motif repeated on Adele Bloch-Bauer's torso. Bloch-Bauer's face and hands are imprisoned within a mass of golden ornament that takes up most of the picture surface. Her heavy-lidded languor, parted lips, claw-like hands and the way her bejewelled choker separates her head from her shoulders, all create a somewhat sinister effect. It was inevitable that such an extreme picture would not find favour with everybody. The critic of the Neues Wiener Tagblatt (a Viennese newspaper) described it as "Mehr blech als Bloch" ("more rubbish than Bloch") and went on to say that Klimt was "master of an extraordinarily developed technique. And what does he use it for? In order to paint a mixture of peacock's tails, mother of pearl, silver scabs, tinsel and snail's paths".

HOPE II

1907-1908
Oil, gold and platinum on canvas, 110.5 x 110.5 cm
The Museum of Modern Art, New York

Klimt returned to the theme of pregnancy with *Hope II*, painted four years after the first version. This version is far less provocative than the 1903 version with its disturbing nudity and challenging stare. This time the bulge of the pregnant belly is decorously covered with a sumptuous fabric. The swollen version of the "eye" motif reinforces the theme of pregnancy and fertility. The mood is less gloomy though death is still present in the form of the half-hidden skull resting on the woman's stomach.

THE KISS

1907-1908
Oil, silver and gold on canvas, 180 x 180 cm
Österreichische Galerie Belvedere, Vienna

Klimt's *The Kiss* of 1908, which has become his best-known picture, was preceded by two other famous versions of the subject by Rodin and Munch. All three show a pre-occupation with Eros and the troubled sexual relations between man and woman that was characteristic of the turn of the century's Western culture. Klimt's *Kiss* is less pessimistic and less misogynistic than Munch's puddle of melted human flesh and less pretentious than Rodin's heroically nude pair of marble lovers.

Of the three though, Klimt's image is the most explicitly sexual with its use of symbolic and erotically charged ornament. An enclosing "female" space is penetrated by the embracing lovers whose combined forms suggest that of an engorged phallus, the streams of gilded spermatazoa-like ornament flooding down to the lower right-hand side of the picture indicate that the moment of climactic ecstasy has just passed.

Despite Klimt's not so oblique treatment of a sexual theme, *The Kiss,* with its sumptuously decorative qualities must have looked reassuringly beautiful beside the harshly expressionistic works of Schiele and Gerstl that were shown with it in the 1908 Kunstschau. For once Klimt's work was received with enthusiasm and it was bought directly from the exhibition by the Austrian state.

THE KISS
(DETAIL)

1907-1908
Oil, silver and gold on canvas, 180 x 180 cm
Österreichische Galerie Belvedere, Vienna

The painting shows a couple that is immersed in an intense kiss. They seem to be posed against a rust-brown background, surrounded by a golden gloriole at the very edge of a cliff or a ledge. She is kneeling and her bare feet cannot find a secure foothold, they hang over the edge into the emptiness; a looming abyss – almost as if meant as a warning. Her legs seem to be entangled in the tendrils of an ivy-like plant. The figures are both kneeling on a meadow covered with flowers. These floral patterns repeat themselves in her dress and in the part of the halo that is behind her. In contrast, his garments are covered with geometric patterns, colored in shades grey, white and black. She embraces him closely and her right hand is caressing his neck, but her fingers seem to be tensed, almost cramped. With her left hand she holds his hand to her cheek. She is subtly applying a measure of pressure. Is she not allowing him to go further and gently touch her lips? His left hand is pulling her head closer to his. Their embrace could not be tighter. Her eyes and lips are closed, she seems to be looking inwards but at the same focusing wholly on his gentle, affectionate caress. Nevertheless her body is showing a certain tension, similar to the tension in her right hand, and her head is slightly inclined away from him; simple passivity or a conscious defensive pose? His head is adorned with a wreath of ivy or maybe even laurels, evoking the image of the crown of a victor. Klimt's depiction of the man, with a strong stature and the dominating posture, could be seen as an allusion to the knight figure in the *Beethoven Frieze* that he completed for the occasion of the 14th exhibition of the Vienna Secession.

DANAË

1907-1908
Oil on canvas, 77 x 83 cm
Private collection

According to Greek mythology, Danaë was the daughter of Acrisius, king of Argos. After an oracle predicted that Danaë's son would kill him, Acrisius imprisoned her in a tower (or in some versions of the story, in a bronze underground chamber). Zeus visited Danaë in the form of a golden rain and impregnated her with Perseus, who, after he had grown to manhood, accidentally killed Acrisius with a discus. Danaë was the subject of one of the most notoriously erotic paintings of the Italian Renaissance by Correggio. Even Correggio's version is surpassed in eroticism by Klimt's. As usual Klimt has exploited mythology merely in order to explore his favourite theme of female sexuality. There is an extraordinary sense of voyeuristic intimacy as we are brought close to the apparently sleeping form of Danaë, curled up and claustrophobically confined by the shape of the canvas as she is impregnated by the shower of erotically charged golden ornament.

KAMMER CASTLE ON THE ATTERSEE I

c. 1908
Oil on canvas, 110 x 110 cm
Narodni Gallery, Prague

While Klimt favoured unusual and elongated formats (often vertical) for many of his figurative paintings, nearly all his landscapes are painted on canvases that form a perfect square rather than the traditional horizontal landscape format In all his landscapes, Klimt is concerned with synthesis and with abstract pattern-making rather than with the faithful recording of natural appearances. Typically Klimt chooses a viewpoint that allows less than a complete view of the castle and its vast bulk appears to be flattened with no more than a thin strip of sky running along the top of the picture.

This picture was another of Klimt's works which show that Impressionists held no interest for him. His theme was the fecundity of nature and nature in all its most pleasurable aspects.

WOMAN IN HAT WITH FEATHER BOA

1909
Oil on canvas, 69 x 55.8 cm
Private collection

The most striking feature of this painting is the huge hat that fills the upper part of the picture and is cut off on the right hand side of the canvas. In the early nineteen hundreds, fashionable women often towered over their male companions, teetering on their high heels, padded and corseted with hair piled high and surmounted with the most outrageous hats. By 1910 this heavily upholstered look was slightly unfashionable by the latest Parisian standards. Under the influence of Leon Bakst's designs for Diaghilev's Ballets Russes, Parisian couturiers such as Paul Poiret had already moved on to turbaned heads and a more streamlined and natural profile for the body. In the *Woman in Hat with Feather Boa* as in the *The Black Feather Hat* both dating from 1910, Klimt seems momentarily to have lost the horror vancui (vanquished horror) that characterises so much of his work. He would soon revert to richly decorated backgrounds, but for a short time at least he experimented with the empty backgrounds favoured by his younger contemporaries Schiele and Kokoschka.

JUDITH II

1909
Oil on canvas, 178 x 46 cm
Galleria d'Arte Moderna di Ca'Pesaro, Venice

Not altogether surprisingly, *Judith II* has often been mistitled as *Salome*. The undulating pose suggests the movements of a dancer and the gorgeously patterned fabrics could easily be Salome's seven veils. It was no doubt paintings such as this that prompted the composer Richard Strauss to make a comparison between Klimt's work and the coruscating score of his operatic masterpiece *Salome*. Indeed the meaning of the Salome and Judith stories was the same for many artists at the turn of the century. That meaning was made shockingly clear in a letter written by the Symbolist painter Gustave Moreau, who had depicted Salome with obsessive frequency:

This bored and fantastic woman, with her animal nature, giving herself the pleasure of seeing her enemy struck down, not a particularly keen one for her because she is so weary of having all her desires satisfied… When I want to render these fine nuances, I do not find them in the subject, but in the nature of women in real life who seek unhealthy emotions and are too stupid even to understand the horror in the most appalling situations.

THE BLACK FEATHER HAT

1910
Oil on canvas, 63 x 79 cm
National Gallery of Modern Art, Rome

Around 1909-1910, Klimt moved on from his "Byzantine" style and abandoned the use of gold and silver. His brushwork became looser and bolder and his work showed an increased response to the remarkable developments in French painting over the previous four decades. The exhibitions of the Secession gave Klimt plenty of opportunity to study modern French painting at first hand. In particular the sixteenth exhibition of the Secession in 1903 presented the work of Manet, Degas, Pissarro, Monet, Renoir, Sisley, Cezanne, Gauguin, Van Gogh, Toulouse-Lautrec, Redon, Denis, Vuillard and Bonnard. Rather like his musical contemporary Puccini, Klimt was an eclectic capable of stealing whatever he needed from the most varied sources and making it his own. In the case of the *The Black Feather Hat*, it was perhaps Toulouse-Lautrec who had the most to offer him. The picture has a poster-like boldness of design. Klimt certainly knew of Lautrec's epoch-making poster of Aristide Bruant with a scarlet muffler cutting across Bruant's chin. As this picture was not a commissioned portrait, Klimt could afford to take a similar liberty with his sitter.

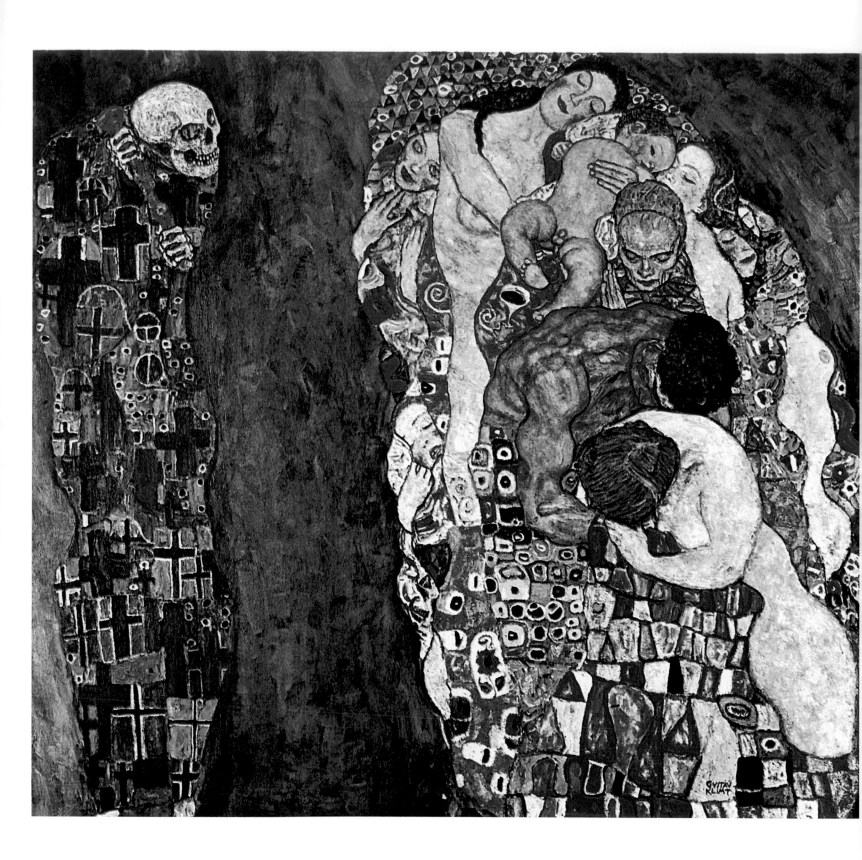

154

LIFE AND DEATH

1910-1915
Oil on canvas, 178 x 198 cm
Leopold Museum, Vienna

Artists of the Symbolist period had a penchant for pompously titled canvases on great universal themes. George Frederick Watts' *Love and Death*, Gauguin's *Where do we come from? What are we? Where are we going to?* Stuck's *Sin* and Munch's *Frieze of Life* are all examples of this. In such a gorgeously decorative work, it is hard to take Klimt's philosophising very seriously. The skeleton draped in a sombre robe decorated with crosses provides a disappointingly banal image, but the floating group of sleeping figures on the right shows no diminution of Klimt's skills as a painter. As in other works where he depicts both male and female nudes, Klimt follows the academic practice (so much derided by Renoir) of differentiating between the skin colour of male and female figures.

GARDEN WITH CRUCIFIX

1911-1912
Oil on canvas, 110 x 110 cm
Burnt in 1945 at Immendorf Castle

This painting which Klimt designed in a square format in the years 1911-1912 but which was destroyed at the end of World War II in 1945, can be classified as Art Nouveau (Jugendstil). The viewer who, confused by the title, expects the typical peasant's garden with neatly aligned flower beds, fruit trees and vegetable patches, will be sorely disappointed by Klimt's creation.

Klimt`s peasant garden is a completely overgrown and almost savage small copse that is populated by scraggy and crooked trees that have been planted far to close to each other thus permitting only a small fraction of daylight to fall in the garden. The ground is abundantly covered with summer wildflowers. The only straight lines in the painting belong to the wooden façade of a barely visible, seemingly deserted cottage in the upper left corner that seems to have once been the garden's shed.

The viewer's eye is quickly caught by the central piece of the painting: a cross, or rather a crucifix that is protected by a small wooden shrine. Painted in a rusty brown and a spotty midnight green it covers the figure of Christ beneath it. The rusty brown back board, which is not visible, is completely covered with blooming, yellow roses, the growth of which covers everything except the two figures. Beneath the feet of the rather conventionally painted Christ, in the midst of all the wild flowers, the mourning figure of Mary stands with her hands folded and her head covered with a blue cloth.

Where may Klimt have found this wild garden that presumably once belonged to a very pious family? Or is it the product of his rich imagination? Either way, this painting is able to enthrall the observant beholder for a long time.

FARMHOUSE IN UPPER AUSTRIA

1911-1912
Oil on canvas, 110 x 110 cm
Private collection

This square landscape painting, part of Klimt's Art Noveau legacy, is presumably depicting the same farmstead that can be seen in the background of *Garden with Crucifix (p. 157)*. For *Farmhouse in Upper Austria*, Klimt chose to change the location and focus on the house itself, choosing a composition that places the building in all its length between two old, moss-covered fruit trees. Both trees have thick foliage and are full of fruit that seem to not have been harvested in a while.

Behind the solid trunk of the apple tree, the big barn door and a small vent opening can be seen. On the right side of the trunk, a bright yellow rosebush, similar to the one seen in *Garden with Crucifix*, is nestled between the tree and the border of the painting. However, the clear focus of the painting is the front of the house. The three small single-sash windows with the solid, wooden shutters, meant to keep out frost and wind in winter, seem to "look" directly at the viewer. A simple makeshift bench – presumably just made out of three rocks and a wooden board – is positioned directly under the windows.

The whole compound seems to be deserted: The aforementioned ripe fruit hasn't been harvested, the blue paint of the façade is peeling off and the diligently covered stack with firewood is almost vanishing behind a bush of wild flowers. Even the windows on the side of the house, above the stack, are nearly covered by plants. The meadow, overgrown with beautiful summer flowers, lacks any sign of either human or animal presence. The overall atmosphere of the painting is one of tranquility.

PORTRAIT OF ADELE BLOCH-BAUER II

1912
Oil on canvas, 190 x 120 cm
Österreichische Galerie Belvedere, Vienna

In 1912 Adele Bloch-Bauer returned to Klimt for a second portrait which in its way is just as spectacular as the first. We see here all the characteristics of Klimt's late portrait style. He has abandoned the use of applied gold and silver but not his love of ornament and his desire to flatten space. The looser, more painterly technique of broken brushwork and the brighter, fresher pallet of colours shows his study of French painting. The oriental figures in the background are also a feature of many of Klimt's later portraits. The influence of Japanese woodblock prints had been visible in Klimt's work from the 1890s, but over the years his interest widened to include many aspects of oriental art. He acquired the full run of Siegfried Bing's pioneering periodical *Le Japon Artistique* (*Artistic Japan*) and collected not only Japanese prints but also oriental ceramics and screens that he displayed in his studio at Hietzing. Motifs such as the oriental horsemen in the background of Adele Bloch-Bauer's portrait were often drawn from the decoration of ceramics.

RIA MUNK ON HER DEATH BED

1912
Oil on canvas, 50 x 50.5 cm

The portrait *Ria Munk on her Deathbed (1912; also known as Ria Munk I)*, which only marginally varies from a square format, comes with a tragic story. The painting shows a young woman who was a close relative of art collector, industrialist and patron of the arts August Lederer and his wife Serena, a good friend of Klimt's. She was engaged to the German writer Hanns Heinz Ewers, who was notorious for his escapades and the scandals that followed. Despite the promise of a substantial dowry, he broke the engagement in a letter to Ria in which he described her as a hopeless romantic and accused her of being out of touch with reality. For Maria, the end of the engagement was an unexpected and heavy blow which led her to commit suicide shortly after Christmas 1911 by taking a revolver and shooting herself in the heart.

Klimt presumably used a photo of the laid out Maria Munk as a template for the painting. The background is held in a dark blue hue which is contrasted by a red carnation that is part of the girdle of flowers that frames the pale face of the young, still beautiful girl. The carnation and her brunette hair accentuate the contrast between her face and the rest of the picture. Only the pillow on which her head is lying seems to have taken on the complexion of her face. The half-opened lips create the impression that she is only lying asleep. Some lighter carnations have been draped at the edge of her pillow and mark the boundary between Ria and the drab covering of her deathbed.

For the sake of completeness it should be mentioned that there are two others portraits of Maria Munk. The *Ria Munk II* painting that was commissioned in 1913 but not accepted by the client and the never completed *Ria Munk III* (1917/1918). Klimt reworked *Ria Munk II* a few years later into the painting *The Dancer*.

PORTRAIT OF MÄDA PRIMAVESI

1912
Oil on canvas, 149.9 x 110.5 cm
The Metropolitan Museum of Art, New York

Klimt had a personal friendship with the Primavesi family and enjoyed their hospitality on many occasions at the estate near Olmutz in Moravia. The Primavesis were typical of the wealthy and cultured Viennese Jewish elite who supported Klimt throughout his career and especially after his split with artistic conservatism. Otto Primavesi was a banker who became the chief backer of the Wiener Werkstätte with which Klimt was also closely associated. Primavesi owned several paintings by Klimt and, like August Lederer, commissioned portraits of both his wife and daughter. The *Portrait of Mäda Primavesi* is exceptional amongst the commissioned portraits of Klimt in showing a young girl. Unlike his protégé Egon Schiele, Klimt was not particularly interested in the sexuality of children and adolescents. Nevertheless in Vienna after the publication of the theories of Freud about child sexuality, such things were certainly discussed in the circles frequented by Klimt. Klimt made a sheet of preparatory studies for this portrait that show diagonal lines converging obsessively on the area of the young girl's genitals, a feature also apparent, if less blatantly so, in the final portrait. Standing with her legs wide apart and her arms behind her back as though hiding something, Mäda Primavesi's gaze is at once confident, self-contained and challenging.

PORTRAIT OF EUGENIA PRIMAVESI

1913
Oil on canvas, 140 x 84 cm
Private collection

Eugenia Primavesi (1874-1963), who used the stage name "Mäda" – which she also passed on to her daughter, was the wife of banker and industrial magnate Otto Primavesi, a descendant of Lombardian immigrants. Their shared art patronage and general obsession with art later lead them to total ruin, especially during the ten years in which Otto led the *Wiener Werkstätten*.

Eugenia, a former actress, was now, in her mid-thirties, in the prime of her life. So it is not a surprise that her husband, still wealthy in 1912, wanted to preserve her beauty in art. He commissioned Klimt to paint a portrait of his wife and, while he was at it, also his nine year old daughter. Klimt first finished the portrait of Mäda Primavesi, the daughter, in the same year.

Klimt made the painting in a nearly life-sized – the portrait of Eugenia ends at her knees – rectangular format and painted the former actress in front of a golden yellow background. This portrait is among the first in which Klimt used the symbol-laden style of portraiture he became famous for later on, and which symbolized a renunciation of classical academic portraiture. He makes use of decorative symbolic elements to emphasise and analyse the psychological depth of the person which he portrays.

The only piece of jewellery that Eugenia wears is her wedding ring. The upper part of her body is positioned in front of an arched recess – maybe a window – that reveals richly coloured flowers on a green background. The curve of the arch corresponds to the form of her head and her rounded shoulders. Her hair is styled according to the latest fashion and she is looking directly at the viewer; open, confident but inapproachable at the same time. Women who want to study acting, considered an objectionable and rather shady profession at that time, had to display an immense self-confidence in justifying their choice of career to their families and relatives. The colourful dress that is embellished with a huge bow in the chest area attests to Eugenia's confidence.

Eugenia outlived her husband, with whom she had four children and shared a lifetime of highs and lows, for nearly four decades before she died in 1963, well advanced in years.

VIRGIN

1913
Oil on canvas, 190 x 200 cm
Narodni Gallery, Prague

In Klimt's late style with bold colours and freer application of paint we see a motif that preoccupied the artist for many years, from the Vienna University ceilings onwards – a mass of floating and intertwined bodies. Here the bodies are all those of young women. The subject is hard to explain as there seems to be no clear symbolic program. The central figure is perhaps the virgin of the title, though her rapt expression and her outstretched arms suggest the awakening of sexual desire rather than virginal innocence. The patterned rendering of flowers is similar to that in Klimt's landscapes of the same period and the extensive use of the Mycenian scroll motif shows that Klimt had not lost his interest in ancient Greek ornament.

MALCESINE ON LAKE GARDA

1913
Oil on canvas, 110 x 110 cm
Burnt in 1945 at Immendorf Castle

In an old dictionary Malcesine is classified as a "small market town in the Venetian province of Verona on the east bank of Lake Garda with a small port and fortifications, population of 2030 people". The small market town, located on the upper eastern part of Lake Garda has evolved into a popular albeit overcrowded, tourist hotspot in the last one hundred years, although the population of Malcesine did not substantially increase correlative to the rise of popularity.

Klimt depicts the historical city center, which has been built around the castle hill, with its closely huddled houses and narrow alleyways. The castle hill itself is dominated by the not completely visible Castello Scaligeri, a small fortress that has been built on the orders of the Scaligeri family, a noble house that ruled Verona during the thirteenth century. The lower half of the castle housed a Venetian garrison throughout the seventeenth century.

The painting is characterized by its earthy colour scheme that features prominently in the walls of the castle and most houses as well as on the shingled roofs. Composition-wise, the painting is framed by the Castello and its looming tower on the upper border and by the lake on the lower border, which creates the overall impression of constriction and narrowness. This is contrasted by the open maquis-covered hills that are visible beyond the roofs and the empty streets at the seafront; the narrowness of the city is opposed by the openness of nature and the tranquillity of the deserted streets. The left half of the painting is filled by the Palazzo dei Capitani, another building from the thirteenth century that was the residence of Malcesine's Venetian rulers, the Capitani del Lago.

Today the boardwalk of Malcesine is the complete opposite of the scene shown in Klimt's painting: instead of the deep serenity, it's rather characterized by the bustling activity that comes in the wake of the tourist season.

PORTRAIT OF ELISABETH BACHOFEN-ECHT

1914
Oil on canvas, 180 x 128 cm
Private collection

Baroness Elisabeth Bachofen-Echt was the daughter of Klimt's most important patron, the industrialist August Lederer. He generously loaned Klimt the 30,000 crowns needed to repay the advance he had received from University of Vienna in order to re-acquire his controversial ceilings. Lederer then bought the panel *Philosophy* from the artist.

With equal generosity of spirit, several years later, Klimt introduced his best patron to the young Egon Schiele who was commissioned to paint Lederer's son Erich and to give the young boy art lessons. Baroness Elisabeth Bachofen-Echt was the second female member of the family painted by Klimt. He had already painted her mother Serena Lederer in 1899 and he would go on to paint her grandmother Charlotte Pulitzer in 1915. The portraits of Serena Lederer and her daughter are in stark contrast with one another. The mother's portrait is a delicate Whistlerian harmony in white, whereas the Baroness' portrait was painted in the riotous colours of Klimt's late manner. As in the *Portrait of Friederike Maria Beer* and the second *Portrait of Adele Bloch-Bauer*, the figures in the background are lifted from the decoration of oriental ceramics.

HOUSES AT UNTERACH ON THE ATTERSEE

1916
Oil on canvas, 110 x 110 cm
Österreichische Galerie Belvedere, Vienna

Klimt began very late in his life to paint landscape paintings but managed to paint fifty-four landscapes nevertheless, among them *Houses at Unterach on the Attersee*. Unterach is a small town whose population has remained constant at 2,000 people for the last century.

The idyllic little town in the Upper Austrian resort *Salzkammergut* was a popular summer retreat destination for Vienna's wealthy upper middle class. Klimt can be counted among those who appreciated the town and traveled there eagerly and often. He spent the summers with the sisters Flöge and especially with his long-time lover Emilie Louise Flöge, a successful fashion designer and co-owner of a fashion store in Vienna.

Klimt only shows a small part of the lakeside town in this painting. The eye of the viewer is almost magically drawn to the crimson façade – the gable end of the house – that is half-hidden by two large trees. On the left side of the house a small dark crimson building, presumably a boathouse, has been erected on the bank reinforcements of the lake. The size of the houses allows for the assumption that their owners are rather well-to-do; the thick growth of trees and bushes gives clues to the humidity of the region. On the hillside, a big yellow house and a small black building that is only recognizable on second sight and may be a garden shed, completes the painting.

The painting was presumably made on a cloudy and dark day. There is no sun and nothing in the painting casts shadows. The colours are muted and blurred, the façades are spotted and there are no open windows. In general, the atmosphere in the painting is rather melancholic and dull. Could that reflect Klimt's inner emotional state?

PORTRAIT OF FRIEDERIKE MARIA BEER

1916
Oil on canvas, 168 x 130 cm
Tel Aviv Museum of Art, Tel Aviv

The youthful, pleasure-loving and cultured Friederike Maria Beer was the only woman in Vienna with the wealth and the good taste to commission both Klimt and Egon Schiele to paint major portraits of her, thus providing a unique point of comparison between the two great Viennese painters. The portrait by the young Schiele dates from 1914 and that of the older Klimt came two years later. Friederike Maria Beer's plump and placid comeliness challenged both artists to make interesting and characteristic pictures. She was neither fatal nor neurotic. Schiele imposed some of his own anorexic nervosity on the healthy young woman. He placed her stretched out on the floor. Seen from above, she is surrounded by emptiness and seems to flail against her fate. To judge from contemporary photographs, Klimt's portrait is more faithful to her personality and physical appearance. He solved the problem of making her slightly bovine calm, and in surrounding her with battling figures, lifted from an oriental vase in the artist's collection. The characteristic flattening and compression of space makes it look as if their swords and lances are plunging into the body of the unconcerned young woman. Klimt's "vanquished horror" could not be more different from the minimalist background of Schiele's portrait.

PATH OF GARDEN AND HENS

1916
Oil on canvas, 110 x 110 cm
Burnt in 1945 at Immendorf Castle

The painting *Garden Path with Hens* was also a part of the collection that fell victim to fleeing SS troops when they burned down Immendorf Castle to prevent it from falling into enemy hands.

The precise location of the setting for the painting is not recognisable. Once more, Klimt uses the square format to create an artwork that is mainly characterized by its symmetric composition. A high-growing cordon of multi-coloured summer flowers leads to a small alcove which accommodates a wooden garden bench and a wooden table. The alcove is almost hidden from view by the dense plant cover that is barely distinguishable from the massive hedge in the background, enclosing the garden. Through the broad gaps in the wooden fence door that is at the back of the alcove, another garden or possibly a continuation of this garden can be seen.

The four peaks of the flower cordon seem to form a silent honour guard for the bright, earthy path that runs up to the alcove. Two hens are standing on the path; the first one crosswise, as if it wanted to block the way for anyone treading the path, the second one stands head-on on the path, seemingly the guardian or tallyman for the alcove. The alignment of the two hens mirrors the alignment of the garden furniture; one is arranged lengthwise, the other crosswise.

This raises the question if the usage of the numbers two and four – two hens, two pieces of furniture, four peaks – is purely incidental or if they have been assigned a secret, symbolic meaning.

THE CHURCH AT UNTERACH ON
THE ATTERSEE

1916
Oil on canvas, 110 x 110 cm
Private collection, Graz

This painting, judging by the unique view on the popular holiday town Unterach, was possibly painted by Klimt from the deck of a row- or sailboat. The central element of the artwork is the local parish church St. Bartholomew. It is possible that Klimt, who was known to enjoy sailing on Lake Attersee, just made a preliminary sketch on the boat that was bound to be rocked by the swell of the lake and finished the actual painting later in his studio. However, a photo that shows Klimt on a terrace, with an easel at the ready, studying the far side of the lake through a telescope, indicates that the intricate painting might also have been created purely on land.

In this view of Unterach, the lower half of the picture is dominated by a small forest of densely growing trailing plants that almost seems to be pressing the neighbouring boathouses and residential buildings to the right border of the painting. Behind the seafront buildings, another bunch of houses stand tightly pressed together. Above all, the mighty and immovable nave rises with its gothic pointed-arch windows. Two of the windows are visible while the third is hidden behind a big tree. The church is overshadowed by the baroque bell tower with its red onion dome that is, however, cut off at the upper border of the painting.

With his painting, Klimt has set a visual monument for the small town of Unterach, an honour that the town returned by dedicating a statue on the town square to Klimt and placing twenty-four small platforms with mounted telescopes around the lake that enable today's art-enthusiast to see Unterach from the same locations that Klimt once used for his paintings.

GIRLFRIENDS
(DETAIL)

1916-1917
Oil on canvas, 99 x 99 cm
Burnt in 1945 at Immendorf Castle

The appearance of this beautiful late work was luckily preserved in a colour photograph before it was destroyed in 1945. Though it is a fantasy, rather than a commissioned portrait. It has much in common with the portraits of Friederike Maria Beer and Baroness Elisabeth Bachofen-Echt in the use of oriental motifs in the background. As with several of Klimt's paintings such as *Water Snakes I* and *II* and *Goldfish* there is more than a hint of lesbianism in *The Girlfriends*. Lesbianism had been a fashionable theme with French writers and artists since the time of Baudelaire and Theophile Gautier and fitted in with Klimt's no-holds-barred exploration of female sexuality.

BABY

1917-1918
Oil on canvas, 110.9 x 110.4 cm
National Gallery of Art, Washington

This painting, which Klimt painted almost at the end of his life, deviates from Klimt's usual canon of motifs. It shows a baby in a cradle. There is no background information on the child or its parents. The baby is, in all likelihood, the product of one of Klimt's numerous relationships with his models since his supposedly platonic relationship to Emilia Flöge leaves much ground for speculation. After Klimt's death, no less than fourteen claims for paternity were submitted by the mothers' of illegitimate children. Only three of these claims were actually acknowledged: two for Maria Zimmer (1879-1975), whom Klimt immortalised in the painting *Schubert at the Piano* (1899), and one for Maria Ucicky whose son Gustav (1899-1961) became most famous for his work as a director of propaganda movies in Austria under the rule of Nazi Germany.

In triangular composition of the painting, the baby is placed at the top of a "pyramid" of thick, richly coloured blankets which seem to be expanding beyond the frame of the cradle. The fact that the baby is so thickly wrapped into the blanket could be interpreted as a sign of deep motherly affection. The little head is resting on a pillow that is covering the rear board of the cradle. The child seems to be happy where it is, judging by the attentive and expectant look at the sight of the (not visible) person at the other end of the cradle.

Despite the uniqueness of this motif among Klimt's other works, it stills takes up a common topic, even if it does so indirectly: the whole spectrum of female sexuality.

ADAM AND EVE
(UNFINISHED)

1917-1918
Oil on canvas, 173 x 60 cm
Österreichische Galerie Belvedere, Vienna

Left unfinished at the time of his death, this painting, perhaps best, suggests the direction in which Klimt might have gone had he lived on into the interwar period. The large, simple volumes of the female nude have a sculptural quality. Like many artists at the end of the First World War, from Picasso and Matisse to Leger and Maillol, Klimt may have been interested in a return to a modern form of classicism and to a calmer and more monumental style. The title of *Adam and Eve* has been chosen to emphasise the primal and universal meaning of this depiction of love between a man and woman. The picture is certainly not in any way an illustration of the biblical story. The plump blonde Eve with her happy and uncomplicated smile is reminiscent more of the phlegmatic Friederike Maria Beer, than of the fin de siècle allures of Adele Bloch-Bauer, suggesting that Klimt's attitude to women may have been in the process of changing as well.

DANCER

1916-1918
Oil on canvas, 180 x 90 cm
Private collection

When he died, Klimt was in the process of transforming this picture from a commissioned portrait that had been rejected by the sitter into something more personal. Once again, it is a picture that hints at new directions in Klimt's work.

The years immediately preceding the First World War saw an unprecedented acceleration of avant-garde tendencies in Western art. The Cubist revolution initiated by Picasso and Braque spread rapidly through the Western World with numerous cutting edge movements including Futurism, Orphism, Contructivism and Vorticism spinning off in all directions. Though Vienna itself was not greatly affected Klimt would only have to have travelled as far as Munich to see some of the most daring experiments of the period. The shifting and tilted perspectives in the lower half of this picture are perhaps the only indications that Klimt might have picked up on some aspects of cubism, had he lived longer.

BRIDE
(UNFINISHED)

1918
Oil on canvas, 166 x 190 cm
Österreichische Galerie Belvedere, Vienna

In January 1918 as the First World War was entering its final bitter year, the fifty-five year old Klimt was stopped by a stroke. A few weeks later he died in hospital of pneumonia. At the time he died, Klimt was working simultaneously on a large number of paintings. These unfinished canvases are extraordinarily revealing of his working methods. We see that unlike the Old Masters, he worked directly on a bare canvas without the benefit of underpaint. We can also see that he worked section by section, beginning with the faces, that are sometimes completed before surrounding sections are even begun. *Bride* reveals a secret that can also be divided from some of Klimt's preparatory drawings – that beneath their gorgeous clothing, Klimt envisaged his female figures nude and in full anatomical detail, including pubic hair.

Perhaps in reaction to the horrors of the war or perhaps just reflecting his own changing attitudes, *Bride* like other late paintings depicts sex in purely celebratory terms and without the dark and menacing qualities of much of his earlier work.

Biography

1862   Gustav Klimt is born in Baumgarten, near Vienna. His father, Ernst Klimt was a gold engraver and his mother, Anna Finster, was a lyric singer.

1876   He enters The School of Arts and Sciences at the Museum of Art and Industry in Vienna. He takes painting classes with Professor Laufberger.

1877   To make money, he takes photographic portraits.

1883   Klimt gets his degree from The School of Arts and Sciences in Vienna. He opens a workshop with one of his brothers (Ernst Klimt) and another painter (Franz Matsch). They create several works together, some of which are frescos for theatres.

1885   The group decorates the Hermes villa and the National Theatre of Fiume.

1887   The Municipal Council of Vienna asks Klimt to paint an interior scene in the ancient imperial theatre.

1888   Klimt completes the painting in the Imperial Theatre. He receives the Golden Cross of Merit.

1889   Klimt begins the decoration of the staircases at the Museum of Art History in Vienna. He receives the Imperial Prize, awarded for the first time to him.

1890   Klimt becomes a member of the Group of Artists in the Plastic Arts in Vienna. With his brother Ernst and Franz Matsch, he is awarded "the highest recognition" for the decoration of the Museum of Art History.

1892   His father and his brother Ernst die.

1893   Klimt takes a trip to Hungary where Duke Esterhazy asks him to paint the Totis theatre.

1894   The Minister of Education asks Klimt and Matsch to do the Faculty Paintings on the ceiling of the hallway in the University of Vienna.

1897   Klimt leaves the Association of Artists in the Plastic Arts in Vienna. Joseph Maria Olbrich, Josef Hoffmann and Klimt found the Vienna Secession and Klimt becomes the Secession's president. Olbrich, Hoffman and Klimt work on the paintings *Philosophy* and *Medicine* for the University.

1898   First exposition of the Vienna Secession and the founding of its magazine: Ver Sacrum. The same year, Klimt becomes a member of the International Society of Painters, Sculptors and Engravers in London and is nominated a corresponding member of the Munich Succession.

1899   He finishes the decoration for the Music Room at the Dumba palace with his paintings *Schubert at the Piano* and *Music*.

1900   He exhibits, next to landscape paintings, his unfinished *Philosophy* in the Secession's house and the painting provokes violent protests. However, he receives a gold medal for this painting at the World Exhibition in Paris.

1901   The exhibition of *Medicine* receives criticism from the press.

1902   The Secession has an exhibition with a presentation of the *Beethoven Frieze*.

1903   A collective exhibition at the Secession with eighty works by Klimt. Klimt takes a trip to Ravenna and Florence.

1905   The order for the Faculty Paintings is cancelled and then bought back. Klimt retires from the Secession and leaves for Berlin where he participates in the Alliance of German Artists Exhibition with fifteen paintings and receives the "Villa Romana" Prize.

1906   Foundation of the Alliance of Austrian Artists (Klimt becomes president of the Alliance in 1912). He becomes an honorary member of the Royal Bavarian Academy of Decorative Arts in Munich.

1907   He finishes the Faculty Paintings and exhibits them in Vienna and Berlin.

1910   He participates in the Venice Biennial.

1911   Participates, with eight paintings, at the International Exhibition of Art in Rome and receives the first prize for *Life and Death*.

1912   Klimt becomes president of the Alliance of Austrian Artists in Rome.

1917   Klimt becomes an honorary member of the Academy of Decorative Arts in Vienna after a chair had been refused four times by the minister.

1918   On January 11th, Klimt suffers a stroke in his Viennese apartment and dies on February 6th, leaving a number of unfinished works.

Index

A

Accomplishment, c.1905-1909   47

Adam and Eve (unfinished), 1917-1918   186

After the Rain, 1899   16

Allegory of Sculpture, 1889   11

Ancient Greek Art I, 1890-1891   77

Auditorium of the Old Burgtheater, 1888   73

B

Baby, 1917-1918   185

The Beethoven Frieze (central panel, detail), 1902   28-29

The Beethoven Frieze:

   Ambition, Compassion and the Knight in Shining Armor (detail), 1902   110

The Beethoven Frieze: Suffering Humanity, Ambition,

   Compassion and the Knight in Shining Armor (left panel, detail), 1902   24

The Beethoven Frieze: The Gorgons (central panel, detail), 1902   25

The Black Feather Hat, 1910   153

Bride (unfinished), 1918   190

C

The Church at Unterach on the Attersee, 1916   181

Compositional project for *Medicine*, 1897-1898   86

Cow Shed, 1899   26

D

Danaë, 1907-1908   145

Dancer, 1916-1918   189

The Death of Juliet, 1886   8

Death's Procession, 1903   37

E

Egyptian Art I (Young Girl with Horus), 1890-1891   13

Egyptian Art II, 1890-1891   12

Exhibition wallpaper for Secession I, 1898 (before censure)   93

F

Fable, 1883   65

Fairy Tale, 1884   35

Farmhouse in Upper Austria, 1911-1912   158

Female Nude Lying Down, study for the *Altar of Dionysos*, 1887-1888   70

Final drawing for *Nuda Veritas*, 1898   30

Final drawing for the allegory of *Sculpture*, 1902-1903   34

Final drawing for the allegory of *Tragedy*, 1897   82

Fish Blood (illustration for the magazine *Ver Sacrum*), 1898   85

Flowing Water, 1898   36

Forest in a Slope Mountain at Unterach on the Attersee, 1917   55

Forest of Beech Trees I, c.1902   114

G

Garden and Summit of a Hill, 1916   54

Garden in Bloom, 1905   57

Garden Landscape, 1906   43

Garden with Crucifix, 1911-1912   157

Girlfriends, 1905   48

Girlfriends (detail), 1916-1917 — 182

Gnawing Sorrow, detail from the second panel of the *Beethoven Frieze*, 1902 — 6

The Golden Knight (Life is a Fight), 1903 — 23

Goldfish, 1902 — 105

Greek Art, 1890-1891 — 12

H

Hope I, 1903 — 117

Hope II, 1907-1908 — 138

Houses at Unterach on the Attersee, 1916 — 174

Hygieia (detail of *Medicine*), 1900-1907 — 134

I

The Idyll, 1884 — 66

Island on the Attersee, c.1901 — 102

J

Judith I, 1901 — 106

Judith II, 1909 — 150

Jurisprudence, 1907 — 31

K

Kammer Castle on the Attersee I, c. 1908 — 146

The Kiss, 1907-1908 — 141

The Kiss (detail), 1907-1908 — 142

L

Leda, 1917 (destroyed)   61

Life and Death, 1910-1915   154

The Love, 1895   78

Lying Lovers, 1908   52

M

Malcesine on Lake Garda, 1913   170

Man's Head Lying Down

   (painting from the ceiling of the Imperial Venetian Theatre), 1886-1888   9

Marie Moll, 1902-1903   33

Medicine, 1900-1907   133

Music, 1901   32

Music I, 1895   81

N

Nuda Veritas, 1899   94

Nuda Veritas (detail), 1899   97

O

Orchard, 1905-1906   42

P

Pallas Athena, 1898   89

The Park, 1909-1910   50

Path of Garden and Hens, 1916 — 178

Pear Tree, 1903 — 39

Pine Forest II, 1901 — 49

Pond at Kammer Castle on the Attersee, 1909 — 51

Portrait of a Woman, 1917-1918 — 60

Portrait of a Woman (possibly Mrs. Heymann), c. 1894 — 14

Portrait of Adele Bloch-Bauer I, 1907 — 137

Portrait of Adele Bloch-Bauer II, 1912 — 161

Portrait of Elisabeth Bachofen-Echt, 1914 — 173

Portrait of Emilie Flöge, 1902 — 113

Portrait of Eugenia Primavesi, 1913 — 166

Portrait of Friederike Maria Beer, 1916 — 177

Portrait of Fritza Riedler, 1906 — 130

Portrait of Gertha Felsovanyi, 1902 — 109

Portrait of Joseph Pembaur, 1890 — 74

Portrait of Mäda Primavesi, 1912 — 165

Portrait of Margaret Stonborough-Wittgenstein, 1905 — 125

Portrait of Sonja Knips, 1898 — 90

Pregnant Nude, Standing, Left Profile, study for *Hope II*, 1907 — 53

R

Ria Munk on Her Death Bed, 1912 — 162

Roses in Trees, 1904 — 38

S

Schubert at Piano, 1899 — 98

Squatting Woman, 1919 — 58

The Stoclet Frieze (detail), 1905-1912   126

Sunflower Garden, c. 1906   129

T

The Theatre of Taormina, 1886-1888   69

The Three Ages of Women, 1905   122

Tree of Life, c.1905-1909   44

Tree of Life (detail), c.1905-1909   18

Two Girls with Oleander, 1890   20-21

Two Lovers, study for the *Beethoven Frieze*, 1901-1902   101

V

Virgin, 1913   169

W

Waiting, c.1905-1909   46

Waiting (detail), c.1905-1909   62

Water Snakes I, 1904-1907   118

Water Snakes II, 1904-1907   121

Water Sprites (Silver Fish), 1899   17

Woman in Hat with Feather Boa, 1909   149

Woman near the Fire, 1897-1898   22

Woman Seated with Open Thighs, 1916   59

Y

Young Girl with a Blue Veil, 1902-1903   41